# PABLO CASALS

# PABLO CASALS

## BY LILLIAN LITTLEHALES

**GREENWOOD PRESS, PUBLISHERS**
WESTPORT, CONNECTICUT

# CONTENTS

# CONTENTS

8

# ILLUSTRATIONS

# INTRODUCTION

THE LONGING to penetrate the mystery of genius is universal. "Upon what meat doth this our Caesar feed, that he is grown so great?" Reflecting on the whence and how and why of Pablo Casals, I welcomed the opportunity of embarking for Spain to see the birthplace and environment of this great musician, and to make a study of his life and work.

Pablo Casals is appreciated and honored wherever music is known and loved. Native of a small Mediterranean town in Spain not far from Barcelona, and proudly heralded son of the province by all Catalonians, he is one of his country's truly great men. All Barcelona takes pride in this high-minded citizen and his name is written in luminous letters across the annals of his birthplace, the humble village of Vendrell. Comrades and friends of Casals' schooldays, who

11

claim with affection "the same home town in which our Pau first opened his eyes and opened his soul," pay eager homage to him at all times, insistently proclaiming, however, that "we who are his brethren know that neither the emerald of the laurel nor the silver of the olive is needed upon the head of our Pau Casals, the real and unique artist who wears within so bright a light of the spirit."

Listening to Casals' cello as he sits on the platform concerned solely with what he has to express musically and showing what one writer calls "an arrogant impersonality," the general public knows little of the intensely intimate quality of his relationship with the people of his homeland. Don Pablo, as he is to his countless friends throughout the country for which he has shown such devotion, has inherited the blended Spanish and French characteristics of his race. Qualities that seem to be marked features of the Catalonians are specially prominent in his make-up: originality of thought, definiteness of purpose, strong love of his fellows, loyalty to family, and singular unworldliness. Endowed also as Casals is with a sense of faithfulness to trust and great breadth of human sympathy, small wonder that on the streets of Vendrell his fellow townsmen hail him with shining eyes, and that when word passes through the village that he is there, men, women, and children from the shops and the homes gather for the greeting they know will be theirs. Does not the inscription displayed in the town's most important shop window—"*Don Pablo Casals Defilló hijo predilecto de esta Villa*"—designate him Vendrell's favorite son?

Only a short time ago on these very streets (where fifty odd years earlier the little boy of four, fair of complexion and not a little mischievous, raced everywhere on his velocipede after school hours) the entire village had united to do him honor. A fete was being given for their great man and all Catalonia joined in paying homage to Casals in Vendrell that day. Special trains had come bearing delegates and members of committees; speeches were made; a street was named for him—Calle Pau Casals—and a tablet was unveiled on the side of the house, Number 4, Calle de Santa Ana, in which he was born: *"Casa Naduia de Pau Casals, Gloria del Mundo Musical—Homenaje de Catalunya, Any 1927."* The "Orquestra Pau Casals" had been brought from Barcelona to play in the village square—the Plaza Pi Margall—and the open-air concert at midday in the decorated and canvas-covered streets, with brilliantly draped balconies and the colorful plaza seething with enthusiastic crowds, made a scene of extraordinary picturesqueness. In the afternoon all who could possibly be contained under the largest roof of Vendrell had assembled to hear one of his coveted cello programs. A presentation was made to him of four handsome volumes, beautifully bound and illuminated, containing twenty thousand signatures of people eager to share in the tribute to him—whole families, including their servants, inscribing their names. These books constituted one of the most interesting exhibits at the great International Exposition in Barcelona in 1929.

One of the men who had known him best since childhood wrote at that time: "With all mankind he has found a brotherhood, and whether he enters the door of a magnificent palace or that of a humble abode, he can say with equal truth, 'I am at home.' More than any documentary parchment certifying noble ancestry, more than any identification card sealed by the police of all the cities of the earth, the cello has made the man of Vendrell a citizen of the world."

Supreme artist and master interpreter of cello music, Casals' recitals bring together people of all ages, all interests, from every field of music—audiences of the elect, indeed.

I wanted to write of this artist, whose reputation lay in so many countries, whose attainments had long scored so heavily in the musical world, and who today commands the eager attention of the finest audiences everywhere; for it seemed to me that the lesson of a life not born to wealth or influential help, yet through courage and character early commanding a world-wide respect, should have something of helpful stimulation to many young artists whose struggles are still in the future.

When I approached Casals on the subject of giving some of the facts of his musical life for publication, he said: "Yes, but you must come to Spain, you must hear me conduct the rehearsals of my orchestra in Barcelona. This is my real joy, what gives me most pleasure; with my orchestra I feel quite free."

With his orchestra as with his cello it is the love of music, not of conducting or playing, that animates him.

I went to Spain twice—first in the summer of 1928 and

again in 1929—and in Barcelona I heard the Pablo Casals Orchestra daily and nightly for weeks in rehearsal and concert. This new manifestation of his great genius served to dispel the hesitation I had so naturally felt at attempting to write about Casals. For not only did it offer a more complete understanding of his incomparable musicianship, but it permitted also a fuller insight into the vital worth and substance of his achievements and into the quality and character of the man himself.

# PREFACE
# TO SECOND EDITION

NINETEEN YEARS later, and again a pilgrimage; this time to southern France, where Pablo Casals now lives in Prades, in Roussillon, at the eastern end of the Pyrenees. Casals, this man of rectitude and principle, whose life has been called "a romance of art, humanity, patriotism and sacrifice," and who has the mind of an artist and the heart of a good man, is in exile from Spain and the Catalonian home of his birth.

During these many years of expatriation he has revealed himself as something more than the artist of universal fame; he has become a champion of liberty for his fellow countrymen, a living example of resistance against dictatorship, and has given his all to the relief of those unfortunate

17

refugees from Spain living in concentration camps in France.

On the occasion of his seventieth birthday—December 29, 1946—Casals received so widespread and demonstrative a recognition of his great gifts and notable service to his fellow men that it now seems time to yield to the many requests that this biography be brought up to date, recording what he has been through because of the Spanish situation and the second World War, and what has been the significance of the rare idealism of his life and work during these recent years.

I wish to acknowledge my indebtedness and offer my thanks to the British Broadcasting Company for their kind permission to use the birthday broadcasts of Sir Adrian Boult and Roberto Gerhard; to Milly Stanfield, acting secretary to Mr. Casals when in England; to Diran Alexanian for the generous permission to quote from his book *Technique of Violoncello Playing*; to Baltazar Samper, Casals' old-time friend, now living in Mexico, who will translate this book into Catalan and Spanish. I want, also, to record my warmest gratitude to my close friends Gladys North and M. D. Herter Norton for assistance more valuable and more prized than can be put into words.

Wilton, Connecticut
April, 1948

# I

# THE STUDENT

Pablo Casals cannot remember when first he was taught music. He learned it as he learned to talk. He could have been nothing but musical in the atmosphere of his home. His world was one of harmony, and from his earliest days he felt life through music.

His father, Carles Casals, musical both by temperament and by vocation, was organist of the church in Vendrell and taught singing and piano. A very modest person, he was a remarkable teacher, possessing to an unusual degree the gift for imparting clearly what he had to offer to his pupils, and, his son says, he would have been a great man had he had a thorough musical education. Of generous enthusiasms, he spread the love of his art throughout his little community. He was always ready to play for and with his friends in any concert of the village where there was a piano or an organ,

19

and his influence became a vital force in the life of Vendrell. Having to earn his living by teaching, it was his pleasure to compose music. He would write *canzonettas*, more serious things also, and then teach his songs to a group of friends and have them sing them in private and in public. He possessed a genius for invention and made mechanics his hobby.

Carles gave Pablo his first lessons in singing and in composition. Casals says that the two people who had the greatest influence on his life, musically, were his father in early years and later, at seventeen in Madrid, Jesus de Monasterio, a teacher who had the rare faculty of explaining the fundamental accents of music, who gave him his real initiation into the literature of the cello and with whom he studied chamber music. With deep feeling he tells how his father's lessons in solfeggio and insistence on his singing in the parish church, thus familiarizing him with the Gregorian chant in childhood, provided the solid base of his whole musical education.

The registered date of Pablo's birth is December 31, 1876, but actually he was born on the twenty-ninth of that month. Casals recounts that for some uncertain reason his father was two days late in reporting to the church, a highly important matter in Catholic countries and one calling for immediate attention; baptism cannot take place until this is done. The birth was registered as of the date the record was handed in. The mother, Senora Pilar Defilló de Casals, who was born in Puerto Rico of Catalonian parents, had one German grandparent, but the father's family name is of pure Catalan ancestry dating back to the sixteenth century. In those early days people took or were given names appropriate to their profession or calling or to some detail in their everyday life. The *casals* in Catalonia were the equivalent of the *châteaux* in France or of England's manor houses, the one big home that each little village points to with pride, and the people of the *casals* were those looked up to. Doña Pilar bore Carles a family of nine sons and two daughters; of all that large home circle three sons are alive. Pablo's two brothers, both younger than he, are Lluís, in Vendrell still, and Enric, living in Barcelona.

The place with which Casals associates the first time that thought ever consciously awakened in his infant mind is the small and primitive *Ermite* of San Salvador near Vendrell. The mother used to visit this simple and lovely old retreat —half chapel, half dwelling—each summer, that her children might have the benefit of the near-by sea. Even today Pablo, for whom early associations always have had value, is stirred by the thought of this tranquil spot, so far removed from worldly care with its atmosphere of restfulness and peace, around which center his first memories of life.

At the age of six, when he had already been singing in his father's choir for two years, Pablo began to write music. His practice in solfeggio had given him such facility that he could transpose any piece of music, no matter how difficult. He had learned to play on the piano, and now at his own request his father gave him lessons on the organ. Soon he was assisting his father and playing the organ in the chapel services.

Meanwhile, he attended the village school regularly, and

in recreation times romped lightheartedly with his school-
mates through all the games of the street.

When only seven or eight Pablo had started to learn the
violin, but his playmates had laughed at him, saying that the
fiddle was no instrument for him and that when he played
he looked like a "blind musician." Truly the child is father
to the man; how many times his present habit of playing
cello with closed eyes and head turned sidewise and a little
lifted has called to mind the same suggestion! But in those
days his boyish spirit could not endure the epithet. In sports
with his boy companions of the village [1] he stood in high
repute, leading them all in racing and high jumping, and the
fact of their ridicule in this was too much for him. He abandoned the violin, but not before he had played upon it once
as soloist in a concert in Vendrell. He remembers that he
played as one of his pieces an *Air with Variations* by Dancla.
Then he felt most undecided what instrument to try next.
Make music he must, his devotion to it imperatively demanded some means of expression.

A group of eccentric musicians called "Los Tres Bemoles,"
The Three Flats, who wandered about from town to town
earning a precarious living by playing in the streets, had
visited Vendrell at about this time. They had all sorts of
rare and strange instruments, guitars, mandolins and bells,
and funny contraptions made of wood and of kitchen uten-
sils, of teapots and cups and glasses, and they even played
on a broom strung up like a cello. These players exercised

[1] I owe some of the facts and anecdotes of the early days in Vendrell to
the kindness of a life-long friend of Mr. Casals, Señor Josep Ramon y Blanc,
printer and publisher of that town.

an absolute fascination over the young Pablo, and when his father Carles built an instrument for him like the broom of the itinerants but improving on it by using a gourd to give sonority, the boy was enchanted. He worked on it until he could play what he cared to of the songs composed by his father for serenades and concerts to his family and friends. This toy instrument, his first cello, Pablo proudly treasured and showed with delight to friends who visited his summer home on the shore of the Mediterranean, the Playa San Salvador.

In a little theater that had been built for the members of the town club of Vendrell, a Christmas performance was given of the Adoration of the Magi (*Pastorets* they called it) and "Paulito" played the Devil's part. At the first rehearsal the music was found to be not satisfactory, not at all appropriate to the spirit of the play, and together the father and son (Pablo being ten years old) composed fourteen or fifteen musical numbers which were a complete success. A few of these songs are still sung in some of the neighboring towns of Vendrell at Christmas time.

Then one day a man belonging to another group of traveling musicians called "Cap Blancs," White Heads, called at Professor Casals' house to ask him to teach him some new dance music. He played the *gralla*, an old Catalonian instrument, short and slender, looking like a small clarinet, with a scale of whole tones only, and while he was waiting for Carles, who was away giving a singing lesson, the small Paulito came into the room, saw the instrument and asked the man to play a scale for him that he might try to copy him. The *graller*, a bit incredulous, did so and Pablo played it after him four or five times, and without further training succeeded in playing all the popular songs that are usually performed by the *gralleres*. It is thought the *gralla* must have come from the Moors—an Arab Pan's pipe—for in Africa instruments of long ago much resembling it have been discovered. Its whole tones are capable of being made into imperfect half tones in the playing, through gradations of wind. The *gralla* is still to be heard in Vendrell on days of *fiesta*. In the early morning its notes awaken the villagers to the fact that a celebration is at hand: first drums heard from the distance, then as they come nearer the sound of the *gralla*, sometimes two or three of them, in a simple chant. As Casals told of this he turned quickly to his piano and played with enthusiasm what he had heard so often from his childhood on. Lovely indeed as one heard it through him—there were no imperfect half tones on his piano!

Shortly after this the Catholic Center of Vendrell organized some stringed-instrument concerts. Three performers there were, the cellist being José Garcia of the Municipal School of Barcelona. At one of these concerts Pablo Casals heard for the first time the instrument which was later to bring him name, fame, and fortune. He was deeply impressed, and thought the cello something extraordinary. Turning to Carles he said: "Father, do you see that instrument? I should like to play it." His father secured a cello for him and gave him his first lesson, and when only a little over eleven years of age Pablo began the serious study of the instrument, in Barcelona, with this same José Garcia.

That thrilling journey to Barcelona he never forgets. He was only eleven and very impressionable, and leaving home for the first time. He took the liveliest interest in everything and let no detail escape him. The rapid movement of the train made him want to run, to fly; he discovered everywhere new faces, and heard talk that presented a new world; a mountain of illusions formed before his eyes. Carles Casals could not leave his work in Vendrell, involving as it did the actual support of the family, so that the devoted mother, who had ever been Paulito's guardian angel, had to go with him to Barcelona. There they boarded with a family of Vendrellians in the Calle de San Francisco.

At the Muncipal School he had piano lessons and studied harmony and counterpoint with Roderedo, the director. For three years he worked hard, his studies advancing with giant strides. His harmony lessons with Roderedo gave him more joy than anything; of all his musical studies composition tempted him most. He won prizes in theory and composition and at the end of each cello term obtained a report which his father proudly displayed in Vendrell, telling his friends how the Maestro Garcia had said that his pupil Pablo could now play the cello better than he could teach him.

The cost of living in the big city, though, was much higher than at home, and there was need that the boy should earn as well as study. He sought and found a position in Gracia a suburb of Barcelona, in the Café Tost. Waltzes, opera fantasies, little solo pieces and some small trios comprised the programs there ordinarily. Pablo, however, always ambitious, eager to establish performances of a higher quality, and early exhibiting his leaning toward the worthwhile in music, proposed a classical program for once a week. The place began to have a sort of musical celebrity, and people came from Barcelona to hear the special programs.

Little by little Pablo gained popularity and name. Attracted by what other people said, Isaac Albéniz went to hear this much talked of young cellist and, becoming even more enthusiastic than his friends, predicted a great future for Casals. After little more than a year Pablo received a better engagement and left the Café Tost for a café in the Plaza de Cataluña, the Café Pajarera, a small round building with glass sides (the word *pajarera* signifying bird cage). Here he had seven players instead of three as before, and he now needed new music, more pieces to play.

When his father came from Vendrell to see him and learned what he wanted, he took Pablo to an old music store down on the Calle Ancha, on the waterfront, and first bought him a large-sized cello—he being tall for his age—and then begged the storekeeper to show him some music. From a bundle handed out to him, Pablo looked over what there was in concerted music and in solo pieces arranged from various operas for cello with piano accompaniment; and finally at the bottom of the pile found the sonatas of Beethoven for cello and piano, and the unaccompanied suites of Bach. When Pablo saw these suites *for cello alone*, he was instantly absorbed by the "mystery of it." He forgot that the purpose of his visit was to make choice of solos and other things to play, and began looking to see what was in these compositions for cello alone. He felt "a terrible attraction" (he was twelve and a half!). Nobody had ever told him there were such things to be played, and his teacher had not even known that unaccompanied suites by Bach existed. He went from the shop in a trance, carrying his precious "discovery" with him, and immediately upon reaching home began to read through these suites. He studied and worked at them every day for ten years, and was nearly twenty-five before he felt he dared play one of them in public.

Casals still says today that he will *always* be studying them. Bach, like Shakespeare, is not to be played at all if not played well. How little young players realize that years of arduous labor and a lifetime of reverent study may underlie the results they revel in when a great artist plays—when a Casals puts sonorous and sensuous beauty, lofty dignity and sheer inspiration and delight into the performance of one of Bach's colossal cello structures. In the early days even the venerated Joseph Joachim used to play but one part of a violin suite by Bach on a program, and Hugo Becker and other cellists would perhaps give their audiences a saraband, a gavotte, or a prelude, as a single number only. Casals it was who proved to other cellists, and to violinists as well, the value of these noble suites to their recital programs.

In trying to explain the inner conviction which gave him the courage to play what no one else would, and made him feel sure that these suites could be made enjoyable and un-derstandable to the public, Casals drew a quaint compari-son, saying that it was like the historic case of Columbus and his egg. Columbus, trying to persuade the Spanish Court to provide funds for his voyage, when asked what proof he could offer that there was land the other side of the far waters, said: "I can prove nothing, it is something I can see; you can't, but here—try this." He brought out an egg and asked the assembled councilors if they could make it stand upon one end. They all tried balancing the egg in vain, and said it was of course an impossibility. Then Columbus with a heavy stroke set the egg down on the crushed end, amid cries of protestation to which he instantly returned: "Oh, I am not saying *how* the thing is to be done, only that I know land is there to be found." He received his funds from the crown—he conquered! Casals played his Bach unaccompanied suites in their entire length and made them beloved and understood.

Albéniz, who not only admired but, in the meantime, had grown strongly attached to the young cellist, now gave the mother friendly advice, telling Señora Casals that she should send her boy to London to study. This Doña Pilar was not ready to do. She thought the time not yet ripe for Pablo to be entirely separated from her: already she sensed what was to be the destiny of her son. The alternative of taking him herself to Madrid, however, fitted in better with her ideas. Over this she reflected long and seriously, and after many visits back and forth to consult with Carles in Vendrell it was decided that Pablo and his mother should go to the capital city. Pablo's cello teacher, José Garcia, was quite sure that sufficient interest could be aroused in Madrid to secure for him a governmental scholarship for study abroad. Albéniz and Ferdinand Arbós had given Pablo letters of introduction to Guilermo, Count of Morphy, who, private secretary to King Alfonso XII until the time of his death, was then councilor to the Queen Mother, Maria Cristina, and tutor to Alfonso XIII. Equipped with this master key, Pablo left Barcelona for Madrid.

Count Morphy took an instant liking to the lad. A genuine lover of music himself, he soon recognized the undoubted genius of Casals, and, feeling an enthusiastic admiration for the boy personally, showed him every possible consideration. Through this advantageous influence at court, arrangements were readily made for Pablo to play at the Royal Palace. He gave several concerts there and some of his own compositions were played, including a string quartet, which the Madrid master, Tomas Bretón, praised highly. The count grew to hold great faith in the young musician's future and a deep personal concern for his well-being. During the two years he lived in Madrid studying composition and chamber music with Jesus de Monasterio and counterpoint with Bretón, the relationship between Pablo and Count Morphy developed into one of deep mutual affection; they remained warm and congenial friends until the death of the count in Switzerland in 1900.

Morphy, who was "like a father" to Pablo in those days, felt that composition ought to be the first concern of the young man. He had great hopes for him and hailed him as the coming writer of Spanish opera. Men like Chapi and Tomas Bretón had thrown off the yoke of the Italian style of writing in which the earlier generation—Chuesco, Jiménez, Valverdez, Cabellero—had composed their *zarzuelos* (light operas), and Bretón had written the first genuinely

Spanish opera. Count Morphy wanted Pablo to follow along that line of work, and in order that he might study composition to this end he was finally given a pension by the queen. Señora Casals received the purse and took her son to Brussels, Pablo carrying with him an introduction to Gevaert, the venerable director of the Brussels Conservatory of Music. Gevaert expressed himself as much surprised that a young man of Pablo's age should have already achieved so good a technique of writing and after a long talk with him said that as his own time was so taken up with his duties as director, and as he felt himself too old to give lessons anyway, he would advise Pablo to go to a larger center for study, perhaps Paris. At the end of the interview Gevaert said to Pablo: "You play cello also? I should like to have our cello teacher hear you." Casals gladly assented and an appointment was made for the following day. Pablo went to the class feeling much impressed by the honor done him, for he knew that the Brussels Conservatory had the reputation of being the chief center of all string playing.

He entered the classroom the next morning unnoticed, sat far back and had the opportunity of hearing the cello pupils play, one after the other, and could observe them well besides. Most of these students had hair shoulder length, while Casals himself, who had no pose of manner and was most modest in appearance, wore his hair cut short. He confessed afterward that he had found the playing that morning "not so extraordinary"!

At the finish of the class lesson the teacher saw Pablo and addressed him with: "You are the little Spaniard? It seems

you play the cello, and the director has asked me to hear
you." "Yes, if you please," from Pablo. "Have you your
cello?" "No, Monsieur." "Can you play one we have here?"
"Yes, I will try." "What will you play?" "Anything you like."
This drew a sarcastic smile from the man who said: "Well,
well, you *must* be remarkable!" Winning a laugh from the
students by this, he was inspired to continue with other
ironical remarks, fairly torturing the sensitive youngster. "So
you can play anything *I* like! Can you play the Servais Concerto?" "Yes." "Romberg? Golterman?" He cited, one after
another, the various concertos and pieces of the regular cello
repertory and Casals' answer being always the same, he said
again: "But you must be *wonderful!*" Then Casals begged
him to please stop making fun of him and let him play, to
which the teacher responded: "Very well, then, let us hear
*Souvenir de Spa.* Now, young gentlemen, we will hear something very surprising from this young man who plays everything." Casals says he felt so shocked, and was so carried out
of himself by his outraged feelings and his desire to give a
lesson in good taste that he began to play without the slightest *trac* (nervousness).

At the first measure of the *Souvenir* teacher and pupils
looked at each other; the students became serious and puz-
zled, and when the piece finished in great brilliance and
Pablo got up, there was absolute silence. The pupils were
looking at the teacher for their cue; but he, the teacher, rose
and said: "Mr. Casals, please come into the other room with
me," and together they went, leaving the group in confusion,
the students ashamed for their master. In the other room

the teacher said to Pablo: "You have a real talent—I hope you will stay with me in class and I promise you, against all rules of the conservatory, that this very year you shall have first prize." Casals replied: "Sir, you have treated me so badly before your pupils that I do not want to stay one minute more." The door was quickly opened for him, and he left. This teacher, the Belgian Jacobs, has been dead some years now, but many times in his life did he sense a punishment for his heedless reception of the boy Casals through those same pupils, who, taking in turn their various places in the professional field, awakened to full realization of the astonishing art of their would-be fellow student of that one day at the Brussels Conservatory of Music.

Casals, not happy anyway in leaving Spain for the first time, discouraged by his experience in Brussels, and depressed by the extremely foggy condition of the weather in Belgium at that season, soon decided to follow the director Gevaert's advice and go to Paris. He stayed but two days in Brussels.

Count Morphy found it hard to believe that Gevaert could have given Pablo advice of such a character and he himself wrote the boy urging him to return to Brussels to study at the conservatory. Pablo, however, answered that it was impossible for him to return; he tried to explain why, but only succeeded in making it appear that it was because he did not like Brussels. In his heart he knew he could not gain from study there. The gradual consciousness of his own great gifts —an awareness of responsibility toward their development —imposed upon him something he could not put into words;

he felt impelled to make the move to Paris. Count Morphy interpreted the step as an act of "indiscipline," sent him word that the pension would have to be foregone, and indicated his personal displeasure. Pablo answered that he was troubled and sorry about it all but that he could not have done otherwise. To Paris accordingly he went to earn his living as best he could.

Again an unselfish mother stood behind the needs of her son. There was a baby boy she had not been able to leave behind and he made a third in the little family for whom Doña Pilar had rented a small apartment in Paris, with the fifty dollars a month she supposed she had to count on from the queen. Now this was withdrawn! Casals says today: "Oh! the suffering and the wonderful way of my mother then. She was a heroine!" Pablo began to look for work at once in Paris. By great good luck he met there a fellow countryman, a man who was later to play in the Casals orchestra in Barcelona.

This man knew of a position vacant in a vaudeville theater and got Pablo a chance to enter the competition for the place, which he won. He was at once installed as second cellist, earning a few francs a day and walking many miles there and back twice daily, carrying his cello with him. After some time the strain began to tell on him; the work was too much. His father sent from Vendrell all the money he could possibly spare, but it seemed to Pablo that his mother deprived herself of everything she needed. She had even made the sacrifice of her beautiful hair to add a few centimes to the little which she was able to earn with her sewing.

33

Again the Pablo ot today pays homage to his mother. "The serenity and calm of that marvelous woman, her abnegation and courageous spirit, ever moved by an ideal which she was eager to have realized, even at the cost of her own flesh and blood!" Her chief concern had been that her boy might not be overtaxed, and she kept up herself that he might never guess how much she had surrendered in leaving her home. Her watchful care lasted until she felt certain her son could tread his own pathway firmly and in health.

After weeks of continuous struggle the climate, the hard work, the scarcity of means, the lack of proper nourishment, worry, the longing for home (in a foreign land and knowing but little of the language), and then actual fever and sickness, forced Pablo to leave Paris and go back to Barcelona. This was the turning point; things fell out exactly right this time. Just as he reached Barcelona his old cello teacher was giving up his work there and was going to Buenos Aires to live, and Casals secured what Garcia was relinquishing—his Municipal School teaching, his private pupils, and his services in church.

From these activities others grew. He played in several churches—the cello now, not the organ as in his childhood days in Vendrell, taught at the conservatory of the Lycée, became first cellist of the opera, formed a string quartet with Crickboom, the Belgian violinist. Later he had a chamber-music organization in which Enrique Granados joined forces with him. They played much in ensemble together. Pablo was then eighteen years of age, and he remained in Barcelona for about three years.

During his first summer in Barcelona he was offered an engagement to play in the Casino of Espinjo in a Portuguese town not far from Oporto, and as there was but little work in Barcelona at that season he gladly accepted. He wrote at once to Madrid to the Count of Morphy, giving him the news of the past year and telling him of this new offer he had just received, and, still regretting the misunderstanding that had arisen in the mind of his old friend over his choice of Paris as the place to pursue his studies, added that as he had to pass through Madrid on his way to Portugal it would be too painful to do so without being allowed the privilege of seeing him again. The count wrote back an affectionate letter, and when Pablo Casals reached Madrid they had a touching reconciliation.

Queen Cristina also received him in her "warm and wonderful way." Pablo played cello at the palace and as he was about to leave, the queen said: "Now, Pablo, I want you to have something of mine, something you can touch." She put her finger on a bracelet she was wearing and said: "Which stone would you like; do you care for this one?" It was a very fine sapphire. This was afterward mounted in Pablo's bow, and remains a cherished souvenir.

In the Casino in Portugal Pablo had a group of six players all season long. This Casino was really a gambling house and attracted people from everywhere in the country. The music there won for him a great reputation. It was later said of him that in early days he "transformed a café into a concert hall and a concert hall into a temple." The success of his programs reached the ears of the Portuguese court, and

35

at the end of the first summer Casals received an invitation from the king and queen to visit the palace in Lisbon. He took train for Lisbon in such excitement that he never thought for a minute about his cello which he had left in the hotel, and when he arrived at the palace at the time set, he found he was expected to play! The royal interest, however, permitted of delay; the cello was sent for, and the postponed performance took place with great success.

In passing through Madrid on his return to Barcelona, Casals had his first opportunity to play as cello soloist with orchestral accompaniment for the Sociedad de Conciertos with Tomas Bretón conducting. He performed the Lalo D Minor Concerto. He was again received by the Queen Mother, who on this occasion made him a gift of a fine Gagliano cello. Some years before, Casals had received from her his first Spanish decoration. She had made him Chevalier of the Cross of Isabel la Católica, and now she bestowed upon him the Order of Carlos III. During his student days in Madrid, Pablo was in the habit of going to the royal palace every week to play cello and improvise on the piano, and the queen, a fair pianist, liked to play piano duets with him. They talked together at great length each week and the Queen Mother grew to feel a warmth of friendship for Pablo which she never failed to express in generous measure. She wanted to give him everything, she wanted to know everything, and she won his fullest confidence; he had no secrets from her. Casals says that he was deeply touched to see how she preserved this wonderful feeling for him right to the very end. Maria Cristina, who had ruled as regent with splendid ability for more than sixteen years, died in the spring of 1929. In her, Spain lost a queen of rare balance and leadership.

When paying his weekly visits to the palace, Pablo was often asked to join in the family games. King Alfonso XIII was but a boy at that time, jubilant and exulting over every new toy. One day when playtime was ended and music had commenced, the boy, surrounded still by his tin soldiers and all the mechanics and implements of a stirring and strategic military game, was so enthralled by them that he could not listen to the music. Casals said to him: "I have observed that Your Majesty does not pay attention to the music," and was answered with childish importance: "Oh, I like it, but I prefer to listen rather than play. To tell the truth—for my taste, give me cannons!" Whether or no Spain's king ever outgrew his boyish attitude toward music, at least the world came to know him as peace-loving and democratic, generous and wholeheartedly devoted to the welfare of the people.

In 1927 Casals had a quite unexpected meeting with the king. The Queen Mother knew that he was touring in the north of Spain and asked her secretary to write and tell him she wanted to see him; he might choose his own time. On the afternoon set, Pablo went to the royal palace and by mistake the major-domo took him to the room of the king. He waited a long time, which was a most unusual thing in the palace where everything was so strict and punctual. Finally announcement was made that the king was coming, and Casals said: "Oh, but I came for the Queen Mother; the king does not expect me." He was told, however, he must surely wait as the king had said he would be happy to see him. He had a short conversation with Alfonso, and was then hurried through to the Queen Mother's apartments where at the gallery door he found the gracious woman waiting impatiently, wondering at the delay.

Back in Barcelona Casals, still the "little Spaniard" in fact and in feeling, worked hard for two years, teaching, practicing, and playing, leading the full life of the increasingly independent musician. When his earnings were large enough for him to leave sufficient money with his mother, he gave up his Barcelona work and set forth to tempt fortune in other fields. Departing for France he carried with him a letter of introduction to the celebrated Charles Lamoureux of Paris, conductor of the well-known orchestra bearing his name.

Casals now spoke French fluently and so approached Paris this time in a spirit of no uncertainty. The city that had seen his first desperate and defeated struggles was now to give him his earliest triumphs, was to start him on that career of prodigious success as virtuoso of the cello which has made his name famous in every quarter of the globe.

Arriving in Paris early in the autumn of 1899 all interested and athrill, at last a citizen of the world at large, his first thought was of meeting the great Lamoureux, and of having a chance to play before him. Bearing the prized letter of introduction, he went at once to the address given and was shown into Lamoureux's private office. Lamoureux was at the moment preparing for a performance of *Tristan und Isolde* in which he was passionately interested, and which was then to be given for the first time in Paris. So absorbed was he in his own work that he could pay but little attention to the young aspirant and received Pablo in a somewhat ungracious way, without even stopping his writing. Pablo said: "Monsieur Lamoureux, I do not want to disturb you, I just came to give you this letter from the Count of Morphy." Lamoureux put aside his work for the moment, read the letter through, and turning to Pablo said: "Well, come tomorrow and bring your cello."

The next morning Pablo presented himself again and found an accompanist awaiting him there, but once more Lamoureux showed the same disinclination to interrupt his work. Without turning his head he grumbled out something about his dislike of being disturbed in what he was doing. Pablo immediately said he would retire, for he hated to intrude, but Lamoureux quickly turned his head (he had a physical disability and could not move his body or his legs easily) and said: "Young man, I like you—*play!*" and returned to his papers. Pablo tuned, got ready slowly and with the pianist commenced his concerto. As soon as he played his first note he saw Lamoureux stop writing and begin a slow movement of rotation, helping himself up laboriously and painfully until he stood facing the players. He remained this way, standing and listening attentively until the end of the performance, then moving forward he embraced the young artist and said simply: "You are going to play in my first concert!" He kept his word and Pablo made his famous debut in Paris in October of that year (1899) with the Lamoureux Orchestra.

# II

# THE ARTIST

CASALS' success in his Paris debut with the Lamoureux Orchestra was phenomenal. Here was a young stranger with no name, nobody knew him, he had no "pull," and he was playing with *Lamoureux*—it was curious! But it was revealing also, and in December of that same year Lamoureux insisted that Casals should play again with his orchestra. This second concert only served to magnify the success he had so instantly won on his first appearance, and to confirm his standing with the Paris public. His place there was now assured, and from this time on engagements multiplied. These early days in Paris were saddened, however, by the death of Lamoureux, who had been his first friend there, in January, 1900, the month following Pablo's second appearance with the Lamoureux Orchestra.

Casals soon began to travel extensively, giving concerts

everywhere, and gradually established himself in the career which was to become so illustrious. In the first years his cello playing won sensational successes. With his facile and clear finger work it was a simple thing for him to play solo pieces of amazing difficulty and brilliancy, and these always aroused the greatest manifestations.

Success of this kind, however, failed to make Casals happy. He did not care to be stamped as a player of showy pieces, and it was entirely characteristic of his devotion to the more serious side of his art that he did what he could to prevent that very success. In England, for example, where in later years he played literally hundreds of times, he can remember having given but one single solo program up to this time. He preferred playing concertos with orchestra, and chamber music, though naturally he was engaged many times to play solos, both publicly and in private, on programs which were arranged by the various musical societies throughout the country.

Having no liking for either the social or the bohemian life of Paris, Casals, much interested in art and literature, passed many quiet months there taking great pleasure in the society of his friends. He had a home of his own in Auteuil, the Villa Molitor, which he retained until 1914. He met and mixed with men of established rank in music, art, science and philosophy, men drawn to that great center by the richness and freedom of its life. In the interesting home of Monsieur and Madame Ménard Dorian, who were his devoted friends, Casals made the acquaintance· of men of political prominence: Briand, Clemenceau, Viviani,

Thomas, Colonel Piquard of the Dreyfus case, and many others.

Even when a youngster Pablo had felt the necessity of knowledge along other lines than music, but outside of school hours there had been little leisure for study. His music took his spare time, he had to exercise, and he loved to walk and swim and play tennis. But in Madrid his friend Count Morphy had helped him with the studies he thought most interesting and valuable, history of art and the Romance languages. Pablo, treated as one of the family, spent many hours at a stretch in the Morphy home, reading aloud to the countess, taking German lessons from the daughter, and being allowed to assist the count in his work of writing, by copying and making translations for him. The count would urge the boy to give form to his own ideas, would correct his copy, and then make him put the same thing in Italian and French. It was an invaluable experience.

One of the earliest impulses of his mental life had been to ask himself: "How can I attack life's important problems?" He had met with many stern conditions in his youth and had had to fight hard for mere existence. Within the circle of his own experience he had seen men struggle blindly, seeking justice in vain. With an intense belief in the spiritual life of mankind, his sensitive mind dwelt on religious and social questions to an almost dangerous degree. The image of himself as a responsible part of the whole weighed heavily on him, and he was carried along a stream of thought which led into very deep waters. As existence became richer for himself through the development of a genius unaccountably his, he was filled with shame over the inequality and unfairness of things, for he thought: I have not deserved more than others. The writings of Karl Marx were a revelation to him, and the study of the Marxian philosophy served only to heighten his own belief that a new social order *must* be evolved. He was passing through a mental crisis and he suffered profoundly. It seemed to him that the sorrows of life were being brought to focus directly upon him and even the thought of suicide entered his head. He had not had the balancing influence of a normal home and of family in the vital years of development.

Now, however, his native strength, his sense of proportion, and his growing companionships with men of broad minds with whom he discussed all imaginable subjects brought him saner values and a simplified conception of the world. Bergson, Sandos, Fauré, Saint-Saëns, Carrière, Degas, Zuloaga, Emanuel Moór, Enesco, Huré, Thibaud, Larrapidi, Harold Bauer, all became in time friends and comrades of Casals.

Bergson and he were "affectionate friends" but Casals says they seldom talked profundities, there were always too many others around. But Bergson used to read bits of his works and ask Pablo's opinion about things. They discussed "line" in music, which interested Bergson tremendously. He said it was impossible to analyze it, that it was a thing both spiritual and physical, and that one must be gifted to feel it. Sandos was a doctor and a spiritualist, a very simple and delightful soul, always talking about worthwhile things, and he had a fertile and vivid imagination. Pablo used to see him nearly every day. Jean Huré, who with a fine literary gift has written much in addition to composing, and whose *Dogma of Music* is a most comprehensive work, was a man of much heart. He delighted in the fascinating game of contradiction for the pleasure of hearing what his opponent would have to say, and Casals recalls many stimulating arguments with him.

Emanuel Moór Casals considered a great genius. He hoped some day to try to write about Moór, with whose life and work he was most intimate, and of whom he had scores of anecdotes. Fantastic in certain ways, inspired in others, Moór always engaged one's interest. He was an inventor, too. The double-keyboard piano of Moór's invention, constructed by Pleyel in London, has been widely played by his wife, Winifred Christie. He made a mechanical stringed instrument containing all the registers from the double bass up to the violin, and a novel kind of cello, looking like a great beetle, which Casals had played and found to have greater sonority than the usual cello though he did not like its quality.

Moór and Casals often played chess together. Moór used to go from Switzerland to Paris once a week regularly to see Casals, to talk with him, play with him and show him his compositions. A most prolific writer, his production was something unbelievable; at each visit he would bring a new symphony, a mass, some songs, a sonata or a trio. Casals believed in him heartily and felt that the world did not give him his just place.

Early in the days of Casals' Paris life Eugène Carrière had painted a strangely penetrative and significant picture of him. Carrière himself preferred it to any portrait he had ever done, with the exception of that of Verlaine. These two saw a great deal of each other, and when Carrière fell mortally ill Casals visited him constantly. The evening before Carrière died, though unable to communicate through speech, he begged by signs for Casals' cello. Casals played for him what he always wanted, Bach, seated by the bedside of his friend in the darkening hour of day and of life. As he finished, Carrière could be seen in silhouette with arms lifted as if in thanks to God for that moment of joy, and by his side his wife, weeping unrestrainedly.

Harold Bauer Casals met when both were at the outset of their careers. It was proposed that they should combine in giving concerts in Spain. A tour was arranged for them, and those first sonata recitals given in Casals' own country marked the beginning of the long years of ensemble playing with which these two incomparable artists delighted musicians the world over. They gave scores of concerts in Holland alone and played together constantly in France, England, Germany and Russia, in the United States and South America.

In Paris Casals became part of a brilliant trio organization with the illustrious French artists Alfred Cortot, pianist, and Jacques Thibaud, violinist, an unrivaled combination. Their eloquent interpretations of the classic literature for piano-trio were the crowning joy of many a musical season in Paris, London, and other European centers. To have heard these men play such models of "artless" beauty as the Schubert B flat, the Beethoven "Geister," and the unso-

45

phisticated little Trio No. 1 of Haydn is to have received a sense of that which is highest and purest in art. At a celebration in Vienna in 1932 he played in two concerts of chamber music with Schnabel, Hubermann and Hindemith. Indeed, Casals takes part in ensemble work whenever possible.

Sir Edward Speyer writes [1] of his visiting at Ridgehurst and being always the first to suggest making music: "I remember his arriving one lovely summer morning in a white flannel suit with a tennis racquet under his arm [2] and announcing: 'Now six sets of tennis first, then the two Brahms Sextets.' In the afternoon there was a triumphant performance of the Sextets, Casals saying that this was the kind of music-making he really enjoyed." On another occasion "Fanny Davis, the English pianist, having just finished playing the Brahms double concerto with Casals and my son Ferdinand, remained seated at the piano and began playfully intoning phrases from the Brahms cello Sonata in F. Casals, with his cello still between his knees, took up the challenge, and the two artists then played the first three movements of the work entirely from memory. For Casals, who must have played the Sonata hundreds of times, this was perhaps no great feat, but it was years since Fanny Davis had played the work, and these two had never done music together before." Casals was so highly impressed by this incident and by her musicianship that he immediately en-

[1] *My Life and Friends*, Cobden Sanderson, London, 1937.
[2] Casals has always cared greatly for sports, especially tennis, and has seen the best players of two generations. A friend once offered to introduce him to Donald Budge and Casals asked excitedly: "Would you *really?*" In 1947 (at seventy-one) he himself played tennis with his godson Pablo Eisenberg on the courts of Prades, the boy being a junior champion.

gaged her to play at one of his own concerts in Barcelona. Her first and brilliantly successful appearance there was followed by others, and on one occasion when she was playing the Brahms B flat Piano Concerto, Casals, in the andante, surrendered his baton to a deputy and himself played the lovely cello solo.

Casals thinks ensemble playing vitally important for all musicians. He says that when he hears a concert artist in a recital program he can readily tell through a certain quality in his musicianship whether or no he has had practice and experience in chamber music.

For ten consecutive seasons Casals played solos in Russia, many times with orchestra; in Petrograd with Siloti conducting, in Moscow with Rachmaninoff; also in Riga, Vilna, Warsaw, and all the old Russian, Austrian, and German-Polish cities. His concert tours also took him through Belgium, Denmark, Rumania, Hungary, Italy and Switzerland. Vienna was one of the last of the European cities he visited with his cello but it became one of his "dearest publics" eventually.

In speaking of his admiration for the role that city has played, he said:

More than any other city in the world Vienna has lived the whole history of music, from the so-called classical to the most modern and enterprising. One would suppose that, after having passed the barrier or border of normal music, let us say, and been thrown into the new processes of experiments, the younger generation of

47

musicians there would have shown their musical tastes and preferences for this style; but that is not the case. The Viennese have, in fact, attained such a degree of what we may call "civilization" in music that although they show appreciation for everything that has been done in later times, they have held and affirmed their love for the music of the great masters of the past. They have not retarded the ascending movement of modern music, on the contrary they have given nourishment to it, but they have firmly enunciated their love of the real thing. Music has no barriers, no nationality. One modern will say Scarlatti is the only old master, another that Couperin is as great as Bach; Rameau was Debussy's love—to whom Beethoven was *le vieux sourd!* But things will adjust themselves; Mozart and Beethoven speak a normal language and we shall rise one day to the point of being able to see the whole as an unbroken panorama of beauty.

Seven or eight years after his establishment in Paris, Casals began his concerts in Vienna and he continued them year after year. An amazing thing happened during his first important solo engagement there with orchestra. He was frightfully nervous beforehand, for he cared specially about doing well in Vienna. After most careful preparation for his first note, he felt his bow slipping from his hand. Instinctively he began a twirling movement with his fingers (a circus performance with a stick, in which as a small boy he was most proficient), hoping to regain proper hold of the bow, but this time he twirled too excitedly and the bow went flying off into the center of the hall, over the heads of the audience, as far as the ninth row. It was picked up and handed back to him row by row in absolute silence. His breathless wait and the interest of watching the slow return of the bow completely overcame his nervousness. He began playing at once and at his very best.

In 1901 Casals traveled to the United States for the first time. He was engaged for a series of eighty concerts with the singer Madame Emma Nevada, but this tour was interrupted in California by a serious accident to the fingers of his left hand which kept him from playing for nearly four months. He remained in San Francisco, and Madame Nevada continued her tour without him. Before leaving San Francisco, however, his hand recovered sufficiently to allow of public performance again, and the cello recital given then made manifest a new artistry: added richness and authority in his playing acquired through the months of enforced quiet.

It was not until 1904 that he came again to America. This time his first appearance was made in New York City with the orchestra of the Metropolitan Opera. He played the Saint-Saëns Concerto, and won an incontrovertible triumph, and later in the same season, as cello soloist in Richard Strauss' symphonic poem *Don Quixote* with the distinguished composer himself conducting, his consummate musicianship awakened recognition of the fact that here was an interpreter without peer. Musical and artistic New York rejoiced and paid tribute to Casals' great genius, but America at large was unready and unaware. The drawing of crowded houses throughout the country was not alone the result of an artist's magnetism but depended somewhat upon "suggestion" on the part of the managers, certain of whom were particularly clever in the art of advertising.

It was the day of long-haired artists; Kubelik, Kocian, and Herr Hollmann were having phenomenal successes. Casals was bald! His lack of hair inspired many amusing remarks among his friends; one announced that the reason Casals had so little hair was that he had given it all to the ladies, and another that Casals had broken the world's record as a bald man. As a matter of fact, an American manager had written to him before the contemplated tour suggesting that if he would wear a wig he could be assured of a much bigger contract!

Inefficient management during this second visit to America prevented the full measure of success due him. It was not surprising, therefore, that in 1913, when the American impresarios were fairly besieging him in their efforts to persuade him to come to America again, he turned a deaf ear. He was not willing to leave Europe, which accorded him so unreserved a success. There was no part of musical Europe where he was not in demand, while in America people did not know him well; Europe paid him the highest honors; here fame came but slowly.

Then at last, in 1915, he returned. Fritz Kreisler, at the zenith of his own career, a hero but just returned wounded from the first World War and with a deeper and warmer place than ever before in the hearts of the American people,

said of Casals' advent: "The King of the Bow has arrived!"
This spontaneous and stirring tribute was like a trumpet call,
a noble and generous flourish announcing the entry of a
valued confrère. From 1915 to 1928, Casals toured the
United States every winter, missing only one season, that
of 1918.

A great disappointment was in store for America in 1929.
Casals was expected here in January of that year but he became ill in Europe and a tour scheduled for Switzerland in
December of 1928 had to be canceled and further travel and
playing were out of the question for some time. It was not
until the following March that he was able to resume his
engagements, when he entered at once upon a series of recital tours which took him through Germany, Austria,
Czechoslovakia and Rumania, and this allowed of his return to Barcelona only in time for the rehearsals and concerts
of his own orchestra in May and June. America was thus
deprived of the cello recitals which had come to play so
essential a part in the artistic life of the country.

Casals now had the same tremendous audiences in America as in Europe, chairs on the stage for the overflow, the
sensational number of encores, students crowding to the
front closely packed against the platform for his final numbers.

He also played many times in chamber music in America.
For a considerable number of years he and Harold Bauer
offered annually a notable series of sonata recitals. In 1917
Bauer, Kreisler, and Casals were heard together in the Triple
Concerto of Beethoven with the New York Symphony Or-

chestra, Walter Damrosch conducting. With the same orchestra, in 1922, Casals and Paul Kochanski played the Brahms Double Concerto.

Much affected by the tragic death of his friend Enrique Granados in the torpedoing of a channel steamer, the *Sussex*, in March 1916, Casals helped to arrange a concert for the benefit of the children of this victim of the "humanitarian" methods of modern warfare, and a New York audience had the unique experience of hearing Ignace Paderewski, Fritz Kreisler, and Pablo Casals in trio—the great B flat of Beethoven. All the musical world and more crowded into the Metropolitan Opera House that night, while many others tried in vain for entrance. It was the first time that Casals and Paderewski had ever played together and the event was one of rare interest.

The musical world also had opportunity for an expression of Pablo Casals' musicianship in another form when, as pianist, he played for his wife, Susan Metcalfe Casals, America's own and much admired *lieder* singer, in her various song recitals. Susan Metcalfe and Pablo Casals were married in New Rochelle, New York, in 1906. They gave concerts together in New York, Boston, Chicago, Washington, Baltimore; in Vienna, Paris, Barcelona, Budapest; throughout the provinces of England; in Mexico, in Havana and many other places. Casals' extraordinary power as accompanist bestowed upon their listeners an exquisite refinement of musical delight, and all those who heard this rare combination of artists counted themselves especially privileged. His own great love of accompanying has provided him with some of his happiest hours. At one time he told his manager, F.C. Coppicus, that he was quite ready to give up his cello; he did not care for concerts any more excepting as accompanist. Nothing had given him greater joy than his piano playing with Susan Metcalfe Casals, for whose artistry he had so great an admiration.

One of Casals' own accompanists was heard to declare that his meeting with Pablo Casals had been the greatest thing that had ever happened in his life and that he would not change places with Paderewski! Casals and his pianists have always been the best of companions.

In New York Edouard Gendron played for Casals, and later Nicholas Mednikoff, formerly of Vitebsk, for whom Casals expressed the warmest friendship and admiration, assisted in his recitals. On the Continent the well-known Conrad Bos frequently accompanied him, while in Central Europe his pianist was always Julius Schulhoff, whom Casals characterized as an "absolutely extraordinary accompanist."

Casals has gladly aided musical interests wherever and whenever possible, many times at personal sacrifice. In England, when Joseph Joachim died and his London concerts came to an end, Edward Speyer, a friend of Brahms, became president of a new society for the continuation of classical concerts. This society met with difficulties and the president and his committee visited Pablo Casals and begged his interest and help. He gave both unstintedly.

In Paris later he used to play every year for the benefit of the orchesteral fund of both the Lamoureux and the Colonne orchestras, giving his services at a time when his fame was filling halls wherever his name was announced. He wanted to help. Generous deeds have always been a source of great satisfaction to Casals. He makes light of what he does for others, saying that the happiness has been all his own at such times; but it is well known that he has often materially aided young artists who have been fortunate enough to encounter on their own uphill journey the great master of their instrument, and that he has not only freely given lessons to certain pupils but has paid their board, and put money into their pockets besides. Once in New York, shortly after the death of a local cellist who had left a large collection of stringed instruments and little else to his family, his widow appealed to Casals to assist in drawing attention to her cellos that she might the more readily find a sale for them. Casals offered to play one, a Bergonzi, in a Philharmonic concert at two days' notice. Despite his own discomfort (for the pegs did not even fit) he played the Schumann Concerto in his own finest style.

Casals visited Mexico in 1919, having a contract for fourteen concerts in that country. He arrived there, however, in terrible times during a period of disorder after the withdrawal of Porfirio Diaz.[3] Rival leaders kept the country in a state of civil war and travel was impossible. His concerts, therefore, were all given within the Federal District, in concert halls, private homes and in Mexico City's enormous

[3] Porfirio Diaz (d. 1915 in Paris), a sort of benevolent despot whose dictatorship of Mexico lasted from 1876 to 1911, with one short break, was compelled to resign immediately after the celebration of the hundredth anniversary of Mexican independence when opposition to his protracted rule culminated in a successful revolution led by Francisco Madero.

bullring—which (the government having forbidden bull-fights) was then utilized for artistic spectacles—José Roca-bruna conducting the orchestra. "They used to come to the hotel before my concert and push my car!" Often he would go out in the evening to the Alameda just to walk under the trees of that lovely parkway and enjoy the open air, not realizing that this was at that time a dangerous thing to do. The proprietor of the hotel was horrified when he heard of these excursions, and thereafter saw to it that Casals had protection.

When Casals learned that the Unión Filarmonica (established in 1910) was in greatly weakened circumstances owing to the stress of the times he at once expressed his willingness to assist, and the president begged him to give a benefit concert. Casals, however, felt that a "benefit" would be like offering charity to the members, which he would feel ashamed to do. "Cooperate with them, yes, for I have always been on comradely terms with the men of the Unión, associating with them as brothers. I have never thought of myself as a virtuoso, but as a musician, and in playing with them as a soloist, with my fee and that of my companions in the orchestra corresponding to our work, I would find myself in harmonious relationship with my fellow members." He later appeared as both conductor and soloist in one of the Philharmonic concerts, given in the Plaza de los Toros (bullring) with fantastic success, both artistically and economically. In good Latin fashion the audience was reported "mad with emotion . . . and left the concert exhausted, overcome . . ."! In conformity with the agreement, his compensation was within the tariff of the Unión. A few days after the concert an envelope was laid before the secretary containing a check for the exact sum received by Casals, with a card which read: "From Pablo Casals, for the hospital fund of the Unión Filarmonica de México. Fraternalmente."

While he was in Mexico Anna Pavlowa gave a series of dance performances in the Theatre Arbeu, one of the last taking the form of a benefit for herself. That night the theater was made gala with flowers and brilliantly illuminated. The *sala* was crowded—all society turned out for it—intellectuals, artists, and musicians. As her closing number she was to give Saint-Saëns' Death of the Swan, always one of her greatest successes. The orchestra began, and where the cello takes up the song of the swan, the tones of the instrument were so warm and the cello part was played with such musicianship that Pavlowa danced in inspired fashion. The audience, fascinated, noticed that the conductor, Smolens, kept his glance insistently on the left wing, also that the first cellist of the orchestra was not playing. The rumor began to circulate that Pablo Casals was playing behind the scenes. Could it be he?—no, it was not—yes, surely yes! The dance finished with a delirium of applause and Pavlowa stood in the center of the proscenium, facing the same left wing and applauding too. Then crossing to the side she drew Casals (in street clothes) forward to share the enthusiastic reception. He would have preferred not to appear, for he considered the applause belonged wholly to the ballerina.

In Brussels, by breaking a custom which had existed from

time immemorial, Casals created a stir which was felt all over musical Europe. The Brussels Conservatory of Music had made a practice of giving the final rehearsal for each concert before an audience and charging admission. This tradition had become tiresome to many artists who, engaged for a single concert, found themselves obliged to play in two, receiving compensation for one only. Every artist since the day of Paganini had bowed to this tradition though deeming it unjust, but Casals was determined to take a stand against it. He was engaged for one of the concerts and came to the rehearsal—a young man full of verve, with a big European name and caring much about other artists, particularly the younger ones, and their difficulties. The auditorium was filled when Casals rehearsed his concerto with the orchestra. He stopped for correction when necessary, talked freely with the conductor, and paid no attention whatever to the audience. To him it was a *rehearsal*. He saw that it was disturbing people, but he knew what he was about, and was doing it on purpose. When it came to the second part of the program, he was told it was time for him to play again. He said: "Oh, no, not at all, I have already practiced my Bach Suite and do not need to rehearse it now." A terrible situation arose. The director argued and Casals defended his point; everyone was asking: "What is the trouble and why must we wait?" and as delay lengthened the audience began shouting. Finally the director said: "Mr. Casals, I am obliged to *beg* you to play your Bach; the audience is expecting it. This means another concert fee and you may consider yourself engaged for the two." Casals played; the papers afterward made a great deal of it. He had won a big point, and had gained the right of the two fees for all other artists. When he was paid he told the conductor and the director that he had acted in protest against a rule that was unjust, and then said: "This, the fee agreed upon, I will keep, but here is the second one you gave me; it must go to the orchestra."

Countless times Casals has taken up arms for other people, but there came a time when he was obliged to take them up on his own behalf. A point was fought out in the law courts of France and Casals lost legally. Even the prosecuting lawyer, however, could not deny the rightness of the theory Casals' advocate put forward in court. It is a rather long story to tell, but briefly: a well-known orchestral conductor in Paris had engaged Casals to play for one of his concerts, and months before had gone over the program with him. The Dvořák cello concerto had been chosen. Casals arrived in Paris from a tour the very morning of the concert and reached the Châtelet just in time for the general public rehearsal for which a large audience had assembled. When it came time for Casals to play, the conductor entered the artist's room in a flustered and excited state, asked Casals what tempos he took, how he played this, how that, all in a most indifferent and halfhearted fashion, the public waiting meanwhile. Suddenly he said to Casals: "This Dvořák! it is quite rotten—not worth the playing—*ce n'est pas la musique!*" Pablo thought the man must be jesting, but soon found that this concerto, which he himself prized so highly and which Brahms had called a "masterpiece," was completely unsympathetic to this leader. In the heated talk that followed the man fairly shouted at Pablo: "If you are a musician you must *know* how bad it is," etc., etc. Pablo, upset by the insult to the concerto and overtired from his journey, broke out with: "I simply *cannot* play now under these conditions. I traveled all night on the train in the hope of play· ing happily for you and now—this concerto that I love—it is impossible. I shall *not* play." There was much argument, the conductor rushing back and forth between the stage and the greenroom, the audience in an uproar. Then Pablo, trembling all over, announced that he was going home. The men of the orchestra came crowding around him, the conductor sent for a *hussier,* who took down a legal declaration, and the next day a process was served on Casals. The tone of the press the following morning was one of greatest indignation against him. In due time the trial was ordered and Pablo did not defend the case. His lawyer argued that an artist doing his work in public was not like one following his profession quietly at home; if he had a disturbance in public he couldn't do himself justice, the shock of what the director had said had incapacitated Casals; that moreover a conductor feeling as this one did could not direct well, and the result could not be of benefit to the public, etc., etc. Casals however was obliged to pay three thousand francs damages plus lawyers' fees. He still thinks the director was in the wrong; says he imagines that he, Casals, had arrived at a bad moment, things not having gone well with the orchestra that morning. Years later this conductor met Alfred Cortot, and said to him: "Do you think that when I see Pablo Casals next he will still hold this against me?" And Cortot answered: "I know Casals well—he never harbors ill feeling and he refuses to remember things that are unfriendly."

In 1927, Casals, planning a Beethoven centenary festival with the Barcelona Orchestra, at which he would give most of Beethoven's important instrumental works, wanted Ysaye to play the Violin Concerto, which he had always played so wonderfully. Ysaye, who was no longer playing in public after the "sad catastrophe" of his last concert in Brussels, said: "Impossible, I have not played it for fourteen years." "Just so—but you can and you will." (It was five months ahead.) Ysaye took Pablo's hands in great emotion and said: "Perhaps the miracle *will* come!"

His son later wrote: "If you could see this dear man practicing every day, slow scales, hours and hours—it makes us weep for the tragedy of it." The time came: the concert was prepared (and Casals prepared the public somewhat also). Ysaye played: sublime things were in his playing despite everything; he had a tumultuous success with a most sympathetic audience. Afterward he was almost like a madman, exclaiming it was a "resurrection," going on his knees to Casals, kissing his hands, weeping. Then he rose to his feet and felt a man again: it was the supreme moment of his life. At the station in Barcelona next day, from the train window Ysaye clasped Casals' hand and as the train began to move he stretched out his arm to prolong the contact, then—it was but a second—and he had left with Casals *his pipe*.

In 1931, at seventy-three, Ysaye died poor. The Belgian government did nothing for his widow who had cared devotedly for him in his declining years, and Casals was later influential in securing certain help for her.

Casals has always been deeply interested in teaching. Of necessity opportunities for work with him, so eagerly sought by students, were greatly limited by the fact that he was seldom in one place long enough to give lessons with any regularity. For several years, however, after the busy winter of travel and concert giving, he was able to arrange for classes to be held each spring at the Ecole Normale de Musique in Paris, and when he gave his lectures there, talking and illustrating points, professional musicians from all fields—violinists, singers, pianists, as keen as the cellists—would gather in the auditorium for the incalculable something there was to be gained from Casals' indication of a way of solving problems of phrasing, of tone proportion or of dynamics.

At the time when Casals felt he could no longer take active part in the work at the Ecole Normale in Paris, he asked Maurice Eisenberg to take over a class and for some time heard the classes himself at regular intervals and gave a course in interpretation. Diran Alexanian had been for long the chief pedagogue in the school, but later Alexanian and Eisenberg deputized for each other when either was away or unable to teach, and when Alexanian left to go to the United States, Eisenberg was appointed professor of cello and the principal representative of Casals at the school.

Pupils and disciples the world over are now disseminating the cardinal doctrines and helping to establish the high standards of this reformer whose ideas have brought such radical and fruitful changes into the very groundwork of cello technique, and whose trenchant scholastic principles have been instrumental in the building up of a wholly new school of cello teaching. It is impossible to lay too great stress upon the significance or the stimulating effect of Casals' ideas, their working out both in theory and in practice. The most active agents in giving expression to this revolutionary method of cello instruction are Diran Alexanian, the friend and condisciple of Casals, who has for many years been head of the Ecole Normale de Musique in Paris, and Lieff Rosanoff in New York.

In the concert field of Europe the celebrated Portuguese artist, Madame Guilhermina Suggia, who studied under Julius Klengel in Leipzig and at seventeen made a brilliant debut in a Gewandhaus concert under Arthur Nikisch, was in her later solo career an exceptional exponent of the qualities intrinsic in Casals' own mode of cello playing, her performance of the works of the old masters manifesting in particular the perfection of her style. Gaspar Cassadó, the Spanish cellist, a Catalonian, worked for many years in Paris under the direction and instruction of Casals. The Dutch cellist Engelbert Roentgen is one of his pupils and good friends. In the American concert field testimony is given to the singular force and power of Casals' influence in the cello playing of Marie Roemaet-Rosanoff, an artist of marked distinction and modesty, the keynote of whose work is high musicianship united to absolute purity of style. Madame Rosanoff first attended the lecture classes of Casals in Paris and later studied privately with him at San Salvador in Spain.

Casals has been the recipient of many honors from his earliest days of cello playing, when in Madrid he received his first decoration from the hands of the Spanish Queen Mother Maria Cristina. This was followed some time later by his second order from the Spanish Crown, and after that he received in rapid succession various other degrees and orders from many countries—the degree of Sciences and Arts in Germany, the Cross of the Commander of Franz Josef in Austria-Hungary, and the further distinction in this latter country of the title of Court Virtuoso. France conceded him the Palme académique and the cross of l'Instruction publique and made him Chevalier of the Légion d'honneur. Rumania made him Commander of the Crown, and Portugal conferred upon him the order of Santiago da Espada, while in Italy he became a member of the Royal Academy of St. Cecilia in Rome. The London Philharmonic Society presented him with the Beethoven Gold Medal with which they had earlier honored such musical personalities as Brahms, Liszt, Rubinstein and Joachim, and made him a gift also of a bust of Beethoven by the sculptor Schaller.

Numerous distinguished painters, etchers, and sculptors have represented Pablo Casals in portraiture: the Frenchmen Carrière, Woog, and Lesage (the last named in the Ecole Normale de Musique of Paris), the Dutch artist Toroop (in the museum at The Hague), and Cases, a Catalonian. Carl Schmutzer, the Viennese artist, made two notable etchings of him, and in the Hispanic Museum of New York City there is the fine bronze bust of Casals, the work of the gifted American sculptress Brenda Putnam. Casals himself likes also the later head of him done in Zurich by the German sculptor Peter Lipman-Wulf. This was a gift to Casals from his Swiss friends and admirers on the occasion of his seventieth birthday.

At different periods of his life Casals has received gifts of violoncellos, two instruments having been left him by the wills of different friends, and a third, a Gagliano, given him by Queen Maria Cristina. Dr. Bonjour of Nantes, a musical amateur and friend, bequeathed his Tononi cello to him, and years later Mrs. Jack Gardner of Boston left him a fine Ruggieri. Mrs. Gardner had tried to give him this instrument long before she died; he had played on it one day in her home, and that same evening Mrs. Gardner went to the hotel in which he was staying in Boston carrying the cello with her and presented it to him. Casals had his magnificent Bergonzi then, an incomparable instrument which he was playing everywhere, and as he thought over Mrs. Gardner's gift he felt that he should not accept it; there might be someone else needing it more than he did. He wrote and expressed his appreciation and thanked Mrs. Gardner for her generosity, explained his feelings and returned the cello. He nevertheless received the Ruggieri after Mrs. Gardner's death through the executors of her will.

Casals styles his cello "Bergonzi-Gofriller," for Gofriller worked always at the house of Bergonzi and all the Gofriller instruments of that time bore the Bergonzi label, Casals' cello being one of the noblest of this cooperation between the two great Italian makers. Once when his own cello was out of condition and much time was needed for the re-

Age 5

Age 16

Age 18

Age 21

Youthful portraits of Pablo Casals

The Ermite, San Salvador

The Angel and the Rabel

Old Roman Quarry

The Casals Fiesta, 1927

Vendrell Scenes

pairing, Casals, who had become interested in trying an absolutely new instrument (a cello made for him from the measurement of his Bergonzi by Laberte at Mirecourt, the traditional center of fiddle makers in France), undertook to use this newly constructed instrument on his travels. In Europe it sounded wonderfully, Casals says. He played it in concerts everywhere and once, at a rehearsal conducted by Eugène Ysaye, the celebrated violinist-conductor turned to Casals and said of his instrument: "Marvelous tone! of course it's a Strad?" Casals smiled, said yes and continued playing, but he afterward showed it to Ysaye who thought it incredible that it could indeed be a brand-new cello. This same Laberte cello he carried across the ocean and played on one of his American tours, but upon reaching the United States the difference in climate affected it sadly; the instrument lost its fine quality, and its extraordinary tone has never since been regained.

With his time broken into by the exigencies of an artistic career, it was always more or less impossible for Casals to settle down anywhere with a sense of home feeling, excepting in summertime, when Spain represented home for him. After the establishment of his orchestra, to which he devoted weeks and months of time and effort, the early spring and late autumn seasons formerly given to Paris and to teaching, were also spent in Barcelona.

# III

## THE SPANISH SETTING

A GREAT art appeals to its own particular and understanding public, a public in many countries and built up of countless nationalities. But any art, and more particularly an interpretive art, includes the subtle psychological factor of personality and a public may be interested to know something of the forces that have been at play behind the life of an artist; may care to know the action and reaction of impressions received in early years, and to reason why the man is what he is. As a tree is a product of its natural soil, so through a great man one may learn the soul, the history, the traditions of a country—its atavism. And art also, like race, may be to some extent a matter of soil; surroundings create feelings which the artist transforms into thought and gives life to, thus creating.

History conditions points of view, and the importance of

what the past has to offer in raw material for the making of the present cannot be overestimated. Pablo Casals born in Russia or in the Balkans would have been essentially different; his base is Spanish. The glorious past of Spain seems remote enough, but the Roman manifestations remaining there today, relics of a power supreme in ages past, and of imperishable strength and beauty, became part of the fiber of Casals' being in his boyhood years and exercised their influence upon him. He absorbed from the monuments, from the marvelous old bridges and the significant and matchless arches, something of a fundamental quality which he could no more put into words than he could his deepest feelings for his mother.

There still exists, not far from Vendrell, a great abandoned stone quarry, the Cantero del Medúl of the ancient Romans, from which was taken all the stone used in the construction of the city of Tarragona (a town of great historical significance in Catalonia) for its cathedral, its cyclopean walls, and the building of its roads. From the ruin of the quarry huge blocks have been hewn, no doubt the last monoliths removed by the Romans, and the flat oblong spaces, layer upon layer in setback formation, look for all the world like giant seats of the gods hung high over the amphitheater into which the hollow below has shaped itself. From the center of this man-made abyss rises a towering and slender column left by the workmen in their excavations as measurement of the depths attained, and every crack and crevice of the vast circle is filled with rich vegetation. Not "the envious tooth of time" shows here, but rather the healing touch of nature, for from each deep wound spring cedar and pine flaunting erect and verdant youth, while blackened cypresses measure height with the granite pillar. Casals one day, penetrating fields and byways to find again this secluded spot almost concealed by the surrounding growth of ages, traveled in spirit the road of his early youth. Transported by this sunbathed scene, so well remembered, with its cool, fresh shadows of trees, he stood there in a blaze of enthusiasm and delight over its primeval beauty, its simplicity and its majesty, and murmured the one word "Beethoven."

Not Rome alone, but Phoenicia, the Goths, the Saracens and the beauty-loving Moors, all have contributed traits and treasures—incredible stores of artistic wealth—to the heritage of Casals' day and age. In the heyday of Spanish power riches had been added through the gold and silver of foreign conquest. Precious stones poured in from Peru and Mexico, and all that skill and imagination could accomplish in the extravagant ornamentation of *palacios*, *castillos*, and *catedrales* was done, and overdone, in those potent days of the nation's prosperity. Centuries had vied with and telescoped each other in the interlacing of the colorful threads of Spanish history—a history that has no analogy. The Middle Ages had been locked up in the mystery of Catholicism of the most rigorous and exclusive order, and after the Armada (that glorious wreck of high endeavor and small attainment) a strange calm had settled over the Peninsula.

It seemed to be almost forgotten by our stirring modern world. Now and then a traveler would go to Spain and bring back a story of ancient Moorish splendor, of mellow old towns marvelously situated whose origins were lost in obscurity, of peasant labor in the fields where the grain was still being winnowed in the wind as in Bible days, of patient panniered donkeys and superb oxen drawing heavy two-wheeled carts strangely suggestive of Roman chariots, of manorial homes of Castilian hidalgos, walls escutcheoned and balconied, with graceful Gothic windows and patios enclosing exquisite gardens. It seemed like a tale of Arabian Nights, so far removed was it from actuality. A certain timeless charm existed there.

And so it still exists, though fresh chapters are unrolling in Iberia's long and varied book of life. Cervantes, Lope de Vega, Calderón, Velásquez, Murillo, El Greco (after centuries of oblivion) and Goya have long been part of the esthetic consciousness of the entire world, and by the end of the nineteenth century new inspiration and new influences had appeared: first an artist in the field of letters or of music, then another with the brush. Distant, haughty Spain had rejoined the family of nations, emerging again through the genius of her sons in the art and literature of our day.

Spain, too, has much to offer in the rich background of her everyday life with its beauty and diversity of landscape, its treasures of contrasting ages, and its harmony of tradition and progress. Ringed with mountains and encircled by seas, the Peninsula has been gifted by nature to an extraordinary degree. While the Sierra Guadarramas, which separate the old Castile from the new, look down upon sunburned, treeless plains, monotonous uplands bare but for clumps of purple heather and endless stretches of strange stern rocks (boulders deposited by ancient glaciers), nevertheless one sees there, through the mind's eye, a rich tapestry of Spanish history and civilization woven by the long line of mystics, poets, sages and other noble spirits bred and nourished in that austere land.

To the north, in Asturias and the Basque provinces, the lofty Cantabrians tell another story: deep gorges and rushing streams; sea-encroaching mountains; fertile valleys green as only Spanish sun can make them; sheer inapproachable cliffs of fantastic shapes and enchanting hues at sunset; gentle slopes thickly wooded with chestnut, oak, and ash, and pathless mountainsides stretching to the snow; while high in "Los Picos de Europa," to which a dizzying road leads up from the Cave at Covadonga where in the eighth century the gallant Pelayo struck the first blow for Christian Spain, two lovely lakes of lapis lazuli lie hidden over five thousand feet above sea level.

To Pablo Casals, however, the boundless spaces of ocean mean more than the mountains; the sea is of more varied beauty and interest to him. Always after a time spent in the hill country he finds something "terribly missing" and begins to look for the sea; it is a necessity with him. In the 1920's he spent his summers at his dearly loved home on the shore of the tideless Mediterranean at San Salvador, midway between Tarragona and Barcelona, with a fine beach and a stretch of water unbelievably blue. He must seriously have needed this only relaxation of the year, for his orchestral concerts in Barcelona in the late spring followed close on the heels of his season of cello engagements in all corners of the earth, and his early autumn orchestral rehearsals and concerts again prefaced the coming winter's strain of travel and recitals. But the recreation months seldom found Pablo Casals idle, and every morning before settling to whatever there might be to accomplish for the day, he had the habit of going first to his piano (this the year round when possible) to play Bach. The preludes and fugues, he says, start his thoughts for the day. Johann Sebastian and the Mediterranean!

These illimitable waters of the Mediterranean gird more than half the coast of Spain, from the extreme northeastern corner of Catalonia where France and Spain touch hands, to the western limit of Andalusia. And in Andalusia the highest mountains of the Peninsula, the Sierra Nevadas, their snow peaks white the year round, send great rivers coursing down to fertilize the valleys and fill the land with rich cornfields, orange gardens, olive groves, and vineyards; even with sugar cane and cotton.

The drives through these southern mountains are superb. It is wonderful enough to travel the roads from Seville to Ronda and thence to Malaga, but the ride from Malaga to Granada through and over the Sierras gives one some of the most glorious scenery of the whole world. Magnificent roads and a powerful car with the most skillful of drivers, however, fail to make breathing comfortable at times when, at great altitude, one's pathway curves sharply around a bend disclosing perilous depths below, while still ahead and yet higher appear other bends and much deeper abysses.

There is a feeling of being suspended over these wild wind-swept spaces where sharp rocks rise and gaunt gray ridges trail their broken and jagged way; then the next turn brings once more a never-to-be-forgotten glimpse of the eternal snows, and fearfulness is lost in the thrill of contemplation.

Roads are surprisingly good everywhere in the Spanish mountain country and especially through the Pyrenees of Catalonia. Great lumbering creaky motor buses use these roads daily, carrying mail as well as mankind from mountain village to mountain village. Far up into the Pyrenees one goes, through narrow valleys where the mountains seem to close in altogether, hugging the sides of torrential streams or crossing them on arched stone bridges built by the Romans, sharing the journey with the native peasant and his inevitable bundle and seeing a primitive life of indescribable piquancy.

Following one valley to its termination the strange little Republic of Andorra is disclosed hidden away between the frontiers of France and Spain. They speak the Catalan language in Andorra. In a very old and rudely quaint house (the "White House" of the Andorrans) there are archives that date back to the time of Charlemagne.

It was a son of Charlemagne who founded one of the early dynasties of Catalonia, "the independent, the delightfully different, the province of enlightened political order," as Havelock Ellis terms it. This colorful land of the Limousin dialect is the country which bred the forefathers of Pablo Casals.

The province of Catalonia breathes an air of vigor and industry. There is a national proverb: *Los Catalanes de las piedras sacan panes*—"the Catalans produce bread from stone." And certainly these people have worked miracles in conquering difficulties and overcoming the handicap of the natural soil. Thanks to continuous irrigation and unceasing hard labor they win bounteous crops from the most unpromising of possibilities. Their olive trees and vineyards produce the finest of oils and wines, and the plains are checkered with flourishing orchards of figs and pomegranates, hazel nuts, oranges and almonds, corkwoods, and carob trees, grazing cattle, and fields given over to the successful cultivation of grain. In various parts of the country curious hill formations and elevated ridges rise with dramatic suddenness straight out of the plain, like the mysterious and mystic Montserrat, legendary home of the Holy Grail. But it is on the old Ampurdan plain, once settled by the Greeks, as ancient coins and archaic Greek vases unearthed there testify, that the richest grapes and the finest timber and livestock are found.

The admixture of antiquity and modernism in Catalonia today is as amazing as it is abiding: on the one hand patriarchal customs, simple pleasures and time-defying traditions, the deepest rooted essentials of life undisturbed by the complexities of this day and age; and on the other a surging spirit of progress and a fast-flowing current of twentieth-century civilization.

Dr. Joseph Trueta, a Catalan surgeon who, after making a great reputation in his own country, worked at Oxford during the second World War, has dedicated to Casals his book *The Spirit of Catalonia.*[1] "Not many people outside of Spain are aware," he writes, "that the essential features of Western Civilization—namely, the democratic parliamentary system of government and the social rules based on mutual consent and respect for human values—found root in this little country placed within the confines of the Iberian Peninsula, and the civilization which sprang from rational experience and the sense of compromise owes not a small debt to Catalonia."

The versatile and socially democratic Catalans have preserved a distinct individuality. Iberian blood is in their veins, and characteristics of conquering races from Greek to Gaul. Despite their determined independence of spirit and insistence on the control of their own relation to the economic life of the rest of Spain, they nevertheless evince much nationalistic feeling. These liberty-loving people revel in their own dialect, a language with a long literary lineage which much resembles the Provençal, and the Catalan poets —from Ramón Lull down—dramatists and scientists have created a splendid literature.

Perhaps in no way does the past reveal its bearing on the present with more special significance than in the *sardana*, the national dance of Catalonia. This piece of pure folk art, with its roots in the very dim past, originating in an earlier form on the ancient Greek plain of Ampurdá, has survived through the ages and is danced today as it has been danced for generations.

Every part of Spain has its typical regional dance and its

[1] Oxford University Press, 1946.

own characteristic accompaniment, music and instruments alike, peculiarly associated with each dance. The Aragonese, in their vigorous *jota,* dance with castanets to the strumming of *guitarricos* with a burst of shrill song at the end of the dance, while in Galicia it is the lovely *muniera,* with its accompanying *gaite.* The Castilian *fandango* and the *soleares* and *seguidillas* of the Andalusians are danced to particularly well-played guitars and skillfully expressive castanets; the ever-graceful gypsies performing their dances, be they sad or merry, in small groups, while other dancers sit around and clap hands and whirl tambourines in a rhythm bafflingly complicated to the unaccustomed ear, making loud weird calls at the same time. Arab influence shows here as in the *cante flamenco.* The greatest exuberance seems to come from the country folk of the Basque provinces on the Bay of Biscay, a people famous for their athletics. They have many forms of expression in their dances and go through their figures with extraordinary agility and with fascinating skill and zest, a *dulsinya* or pipe intoning while someone beats a board with tomtom-like effect. Occasionally they make use of a concertina in their accompaniments, a tambourine too. The *zorzico* is a typical Basque dance, though the *aurresku* for eight dancers is the most famous and bears resemblance to some primitive rite.

But of all Spanish dances the *sardana* of Catalonia seems to be the most symbolic of national consciousness, seems to have the deepest and most living impulse. Danced always in the open air, it has become an essential part of the communal life of the people. Casals says that one can scarcely overstress the value of the *sardana* to the Catalans and that a stranger can have no idea of how much the dance means to them. To quote him: "It is the expression of a strength the people feel within themselves; when they dance the *sardana* they are conscious of their country, their families, their soil, and everything that is strong in life. Then besides there is the musical importance of the *sardana*, as the real beginning of Spanish musical expression in composition. This dance form has the relation to modern Spanish music that the minuet and saraband had to the music of the classic composers."

The music of the *sardana* is written for a *cobla*, or ensemble, of strident *tenoras*, *tiples*, and *fluviol* (quite ancient wood-wind instruments peculiar to Catalonia), trumpets, flishorn, and a double bass, with often a diminutive drum tapped by the player of the fluviol. Always there is an introductory flourish from the fluviol, a high-pitched, primitive sort of piccolo, which runs as follows:

The *sardana* is announced and the *cobla* begins one of the hundreds of pieces always on hand. At the first sound of these vibrant instruments dancers gather and groups commence to form. In a short time circles become large as one person after another—young and old alike—breaks in, joins hands in a most impersonal fashion, and falls into the swinging movement, left to right, and the rhythm of the step. In all dancing centers there are groups without number, circle after circle, and circle within circle; it may be of men alone, of girls only, or composed of both men and girls—it seems to matter little which. The dance is slow, measured, methodical; it begins and ends deliberately. Rodin has said that "slowness is beauty"; and it is true that the grave and serious measures of the *sardana* seem to weave a spell of peculiar charm and fascination over the onlooker.

Before the actual dance begins, the music is played once through by the *cobla* that the dancers may first feel the rhythm. Nevertheless it puzzles the onlooker to understand why they should all be able to make the various movements— left to right, right to left—and the involved changes of step so completely in unison as they do, for one looks in vain for evidence of leadership. They say there is a leader—one dancer in each group whom the others follow. Perhaps the ring of hands clasped, somewhat lifted and in constant up and down movement in a quick rhythmic motion, consti- tutes a sensitized line of communication between heads and heels! A *sardana* may be found and seen, anywhere, every- where, always, late afternoon and nights, Sunday mornings and on days of *fiesta*. It may be danced on the broad street of the Paralelo (the Bowery of Barcelona) where tables and chairs line the sidewalks for blocks, and people eat and drink in between dances; or it may be watched in the parks and public squares of any city, town, or hamlet in the whole province of Catalonia. It is to be seen at times danced on the hard sands of the beaches at seaside places, and there are special occasions when whole villages turn out to dance on the chosen evening, everything else being laid aside for it. The people constitute both audience and performers, and the stranger at these gatherings, the outside spectator of the dance, sitting, standing, or walking among the crowds, somehow feels himself in very happy relation with it all.

If a peasant in Catalonia has any instinct for music he writes a *sardana* and most native composers have commenced with this dance and through it have worked up to the symphonic form. Some of them, like Juli Garreta whose *sardanas* are among the finest and most frequently played in the country, have written symphonies of a very high type.

Garreta of San Feliu, who died in 1925 in the prime of young manhood, began work as an ordinary day laborer and then became a watchmaker, but gave his greatest interest to music though he had never had a lesson in his life. He had never visited a big town, nor had he even heard any music except for a little piano playing, but he had the love of it in his heart and an intuitive gift, and felt at an early age that he must compose. He wrote hundreds of *sardanas*—his truest form of expression—and composed sonatas, quartets, symphonic poems and symphonies. Many of his orchestral things, which Casals calls "original and wholly musical," were performed in Barcelona by the Casals Orchestra.

The most noted composer of these dances since the time of "old man Pep Ventura" a hundred years ago is Morera, while Manén the violinist, Todrá, Pujol, and Lamotte de Grignon have been especially fruitful in their writing for this particular form of folk expression. Casals' brother Enric, too, has become celebrated for his modern *sardanas*, while

Pablo's own "Festivola" is one of the most popular of all.

Spain has another form of dance expression, slower than the *sardana* and still more stately in movement. *Los seises,* a dance belonging to the church ritual, of origin unknown, is performed at vesper service before the high altar in the Cathedral at Seville, twice each year as part of the religious ceremony in times of special ecclesiastical celebration, during the "octave," or eight days, of Corpus Christi and that of the Immaculate Conception. Ten boys, not six as the name would indicate, dressed in costume and wearing plumed hats throughout the dance, face each other, singing and playing castanets, while they go through their devotional evolutions to the accompaniment of a full orchestra.

Despite all the outward form and ritual of the Catholic church in Spain, there is an element of great simplicity in the worship there, and when one realizes the church service as a daily (indeed an hourly) emotional response to the inner need of thousands of impressionable men and women, rich and poor alike, one begins to comprehend something of the faith of these people. Only the symbols have grown old; the spiritual essence remains. One author writes of "the supreme manifestation of a certain primitive and eternal attitude of the human spirit in Spain, an attitude of spiritual exaltation and heroic energy directed not chiefly toward comfort or gain but toward the more fundamental facts of human existence"; while Keyserling, in indicating what Spain could mean to a world endeavoring to develop an age of more spiritual quality, has said—"To me there is no doubt that, ethically, Spain stands at the head of European mankind today." Strange words to read in 1948!—Another far-seeing writer, Angel Ganivet, has visualized Spain as "the apostle of future ideas"—and this a country in which one may plunge backward fifteen or twenty thousand years before Christ, to find on the walls of the Caves of Altamira polychrome frescos of animals—bison, boar, stag, and wild horse—intact and well-preserved, painted by prehistoric man in the days when the world was in the grip of an ice age.

Many famous men are claimed by different Catalonian writers as offspring of their motherland. One Ulloa, in *Colomb Catalá*, proves, to his own satisfaction at least, that Christopher Columbus was a Catalonian, native of the town of Genova on the Island of Majorca, where the name Colomb is still borne by many families. The scene of pirate raids for centuries, Majorca was captured by the Catalans under the Count of Barcelona in the twelfth century; and indeed, within a hundred years all the Balearic Islands were conquered by Jaime I, King of Aragon and Count of Barcelona, suffering strange vicissitudes and many changes of ruling power, until in 1802 Great Britain ceded them back to Spain by the treaty of Amiens. Another writer declares that several far-removed great-greats in the line of Napoleon Bonaparte's paternal grandparents lived for one hundred and twenty-four years on this same lovely island—where twisted and bulbous olive trees over one thousand years old are still bearing fruit—before the family moved to Corsica. Even the Cabots of Boston are said to have historical roots there! Whatever the truth of these assertions, the romantic medieval figure of Ramón Lull, the "Doctor Illuminatus" of the

Catalans and their first great poet, classed among the famous scholars of all time, shines forth in fullest authenticity as a son of proud Palma, Majorca's chief city.

Across the waters, but a short night's steamer trip from Palma, lies Barcelona, the capital of Catalonia and the home of Pablo Casals. This old Roman city occupies one of the loveliest sites on the shores of the Mediterranean. It has much older and deeper roots than Madrid, the present seat of the Spanish government. It was here that his royal sponsors, Ferdinand and Isabella, received Columbus and created him Lord High Admiral of the Indies upon his return (overland from Palos) from his epoch-making voyage; and there now stands, looking out over the bay, a lofty column capped by a statue, one arm stretched out toward the distant land of his discovery, of this mariner who helped make Spain mistress of a great part of the world.

The view of the city with its shapely harbor seen from the heights of Mt. Tibidabo to the north is superb; at nighttime it is simply unforgettable. The blaze of bright light from the town as it lies cupped between the two hills, Tibidabo and Montjuic, is impressively beautiful in itself any night after dark, but when there chances to be a great Spanish exposition—as in the summer of 1929—illuminating the entire hillside of Montjuic almost down to the water's edge, the myriad reflections and the dazzling flood of light produce an effect almost too startling and too vivid to seem real.

Spain's transition from medievalism to modernism is nowhere more clearly exemplified than in Barcelona. In the old Barcelona that Cervantes loved one can still realize the land of ancient heroic enterprise and, while the new section of the city is a model of present-day business accomplishment, it yet remains an integral part of the whole. Barcelona has been the mecca of traders from earliest times, and today is the center of an intense activity in mercantile and maritime affairs. Rapid in its growth of material prosperity, this handsome and well-regulated city has a population of close to a million and a quarter and possesses one of the most up-to-date subway systems in the world, as well as a completely modern telephone system.

Wide arteries have been opened for traffic in some of the oldest parts of the town, but the most precious relics of antiquity have been preserved—links that bind today and the existing order of things to the misty Middle Ages and times still more remote. Two of the most interesting old monuments of Spanish religious architecture still stand there: the mystical tenth-century monastery of San Pablo del Campo, with its small cloisters of delightful originality, and the splendid Gothic cathedral, superb in its severity, with a noble simplicity and firmness of proportion and a wealth of beautiful stained-glass windows. One may wander at night through the miles of curving passageways and incredibly narrow streets surrounding the cathedral, many of them hung with lighted lanterns their entire length; and in some of the dim alleyways may meet with old men wearing greatcoats to their heels, queer hats on their heads, keys dangling and clanking, and bearing on poles over their shoulders the curiously wrought lanterns of other days.

There is a public monument in Barcelona to the musician José Anselmo Clavé, and Casals' face lighted up with pleasure as he told who this man was. He said it was absolutely necessary for an understanding of Spain's present-day musical situation to know what Clavé had done for Catalonia, adding that his own association of concerts for workingmen was but a natural outgrowth of Clavé's momentous efforts in earlier years. A weaver, and a born genius, Clavé accomplished a great work throughout his province, a work of "salvation by music," as Casals put it; and the present-day distinguished singing societies of long standing, the Orfeos Catalá and Gracienc, as well as the numerous other choirs and choruses of Barcelona, are the direct inheritors of the Clavé tradition.

A great lover of his fellows, Clavé had the fullest understanding of the temptations that beset men transplanted from the free and communal life of pre-industrial times in the country to the big towns and cities with their factories, their division of rich and poor and other attestations of economic change. He well knew how easy it was for these men in strange surroundings, with no ties between themselves and their neighbors, to find comfort in the wine cellars and public houses of Barcelona; but the degradation of such a life he refused to admit as necessary or as a thing impossible of betterment. A lover of music himself, he cast about in his mind for a way of interesting his fellow workmen in it too. He was entirely untaught but could improvise well on the guitar, could sing, and was ready with both words and music in composing songs.

He first tried to gain the men's attention with his own singing and playing, then found out which men had good voices and for them wrote special songs. They seemed to find entertainment and pleasure in this, and he redoubled his efforts. Interest increased and expanded, many groups relinquishing old habits and turning to Clavé for music after work hours. A meeting of men in one factory would lead to the formation of a group in another, Clavé's influence spreading from district to district throughout the city. Years later there was scarcely a small town in the province which had not at least one choir of workingmen as a direct result of this pioneer work.

Clavé, born in 1830 in most humble circumstances, lived to be made Governor of Tarragona. He was powerful and intelligent, with an unlimited enthusiasm and an enormous capacity for work. One secret of his force lay in the surging spirit of joy manifest in him with every new point he gained for others. Possessing a strongly poetic quality, the songs which bore his words were really lovely. In them he exploited the deepest feelings of the workingmen, putting into both words and music his conception of the elemental affections. He took all the healthy emotions and exalted them; love, love of home, chivalry and patriotism. His musical ideas began taking hold all over the country, and with an ever-widening field to work in, he composed choral works of a much more important order. He would write for the farmers songs of the harvest time and others expressive of nature and her creations, and for the fishermen he produced "marvelous marine epics," all this becoming a valuable stimulus to the

culture of Catalonia. His potent and fertile influence on the
working people of the province at a time of great political un-
rest was acknowledged by a government forced to recognize
the strength and importance of his work. After his death in
Barcelona in 1874, the city erected this statue to his memory
in the Plaza de Cataluña.

The standard of music in Barcelona in 1929 was high. The
opera was of front rank, and in Europe the securing of an
advantageous appearance there counted greatly in a young
singer's favor. A triumph at La Scala in Milan and a success
scored in the Lycée of Barcelona were considered the turning
points in the career of an opera singer.

With a network of societies devoted to chamber music all
over the peninsula, perhaps the most important private musical organization of Spain was the Camera de Música in Barcelona. It outranked most of the others in the number and
quality of the concerts for which it was responsible. It
engaged every famous artist possible to secure, sometimes
spending as much as six thousand dollars on a single concert,
and Casals thought that no one other chamber-music society
in the world presented the interest and variety of program
that it did each year.

The society began as an amateur affair, a weekly reunion
of friends who used to play for and with each other. A small
orchestra was formed, half professional and half amateur;
then someone said: "Why not make a society of it and
charge a membership fee?" It did not thrive, however, and
the leader of the little orchestra, who was a pupil of his,
spoke to Casals and asked his advice as to programs, etc. The

whole idea was quite sympathetic to Casals and he offered his services to the society for a concert. It had been almost ten years since he had played cello publicly in Barcelona, and his great European reputation had made the city proud of him and eager to hear him again, so that everyone was keyed up to a high pitch of expectancy. As it was a private society and no tickets could be bought, people had to become members to obtain admission, and before that one concert nearly six hundred new members were enrolled. That was the beginning of its great success as an organization. It became fashionable and "the thing" to belong; the people fairly rushed to join. The society grew too quickly and became too social, with the result that at the concerts much talking was indulged in, a vice it has seemed impossible to curb. Despite the emphatic protests of the dyed-in-the-wool lovers of music, these concerts remained social reunions in the true sense of the word, and the various colonies (composed of summertime seaside neighbors and the like), forming groups in the concert hall, had so much else to interest them that at times they found it very hard to listen to the music!

The Camera de Música gave two concerts a week for a season of eight weeks, and Casals played for it frequently. The society stood behind the Casals Orchestra, engaged it for concerts and contributed yearly to its maintenance. The Camera engaged all the greatest artists of the world, from Paderewski and Kreisler on through the long list of eminent soloists; had programs of orchestral, quartet and trio music, and arranged for appearances of such noted composers as Stravinsky, Schönberg, Ravel, Milhaud, Honegger and Moór.

They also gave interesting performances of old Italian operas with the assistance of the two Orfeos, Catalá and Gracienc.

The Camera, however, was not the only serious chamber-music society in Barcelona. There was also the "Amics" (a friends-of-music society) with about two hundred members and a not very strong financial position. They gave of the finest in music and kept up their beloved organization for the pure love of it. No talking allowed in concerts of the Amics!

# IV

## THE ORQUESTRA
## PAU CASALS

WALKING to the Palacio de la Música Catalana of a late
spring evening, and passing through some of Barcelona's
oldest and narrowest streets, one suddenly comes out on the
Via Layetana, a wide, well-lighted avenue, busy and noisy—
a startling contrast of the vital present with the sleepy past
—and one feels a most un-Spanish sense of haste. But there
is no need of hurry; concerts do not begin in Barcelona until
ten o'clock or later!

At the corner of Alta de San Pedro, stands the immense
ultra-modern structure of Doménech and Muntaner, the
Catalonian architects, built as a home for the Orfeo Catalá,
its façade ornamented by a colossal group of statuary—"Popular Song" by the sculptor Blay—and at the entrance door

huge billboards announcing the concert of the "Orquestra Pau Casals." This Palace of Music holds a fine concert hall, large, well proportioned and perfect acoustically (unhappily overdecorated), and here Pablo Casals gave a series of symphony concerts every spring and fall.

The playing of the Casals Orchestra in Barcelona was a complete revelation. Even with a full comprehension beforehand of Casals' greatness as musician and interpreter, this further demonstration of his artistic activity shed a new light upon his manifold genius. To hear how he won from that group of men (few of them players of more than ordinary ability) finished results that the highest type of metropolitan orchestra might well be proud of was to learn, in a new way, the colossal stature of the man, musically. It made one only thankful that his ardent desire, expressed in youth in a letter to a friend, should have finally found such definite fulfillment. In the first flush of triumph as a virtuoso with his cello he had written: *"Si j'ai été si heureux jusqu'à présent en raclant* [scratching] *le violoncelle, comme je serai heureux quand je possèderai le plus grand instrument, l'orchestre!"*

And he did indeed "possess" his orchestra; his refusal to compromise in working for the high mark set, his profoundly human and understanding attitude toward the efforts of the musicians, and the magnetism of his own simple, direct, and almost childlike friendliness, won for him the enthusiastic affection, respect, and allegiance of every man in the orchestra. Continuous training, rehearsals without number, and a generous giving of time, heart, brain and energy on the part of the leader made possible the observance of both the spirit and the letter in the Pablo Casals Orchestra. For nine years Casals worked with this group of men and he created an orchestra of the first class and rank. In all parts of Europe one heard the cry: "Inadequate financial backing! lack of rehearsals! how can a point of technical perfection be attained?" The truth is that during those years Casals himself supplied the financial backing and gave the necessary rehearsals.

He had a legitimate feeling of pride in his splendid orchestra. It was an instrument upon which he played, conducting with decisive, plastic and highly expressive beat, and communicating to the listener a musical speech that breathed the breath of life. There was no effort at virtuoso conducting; the remarkable perfection attained was due to hard work, perseverance and enthusiasm. Pablo Casals said: "We just make music"; but he fired his men with the sacred contagion of his own respect and love for what he played, and instilled into the body of his organization all the essential qualities of musicianship. He gave a matchless interpretation of the Schubert C Major Symphony in Barcelona in June 1928, the memory of which will long remain an inspiration and a joy to those who heard it. Under deep emotional influence when he reads this ineffable score, something almost Attic in his sense of delicacy and restraint keeps him always within the confines of his art, and in the deathless beauty and wonder of this work he achieves, what only a great musician and conductor can achieve, a genuine Schubert simplicity.

All the musicians in the orchestra showed that they felt the inspiration, and the power, of Casals at the baton. He talked points over with them, and encouraged them to discuss things among themselves. He listened to what they had to say, and explained his own reasons for certain decisions; for, while essentially a leader, he believes heartily in cooperation.

It is interesting to learn Casals' methods of approach in working with the orchestra in the first days of its establishment. He found the men more or less confirmed in careless ways of playing, owing to the impossibility of their ever having rehearsals enough for their performances at the opera or for any other orchestral undertakings. So he talked to them seriously, and explained that they would learn better the value of musical articulation if they set themselves some regular and deliberate orchestral exercise. Selecting Wagner's Ride of the Valkyries he started work of so exhaustive and forceful a nature—phrase by phrase, run by run, slower and slower, beaten out with meticulous care in absolute rhythm and with insistent clarity—that his motto of "honesty to the limit" was well driven home through finger, arm and brain, to the very soul of each man.

All the string players were given an insight into Casals' unique ways of bowing and fingering; indeed, every member of the orchestra was made to respond individually to his most exacting musical demands, and even the drum player felt an intimate touch with the compelling force of this leader. The result in performance was great beauty of line, suavity of phrasing, fullest dynamic and rhythmic values, and satisfying equilibrium of tone, with an achievement of sustained pianissimo transcendental in quality.

Casals is never more at ease than with the men of his orchestra, and especially does he love the intimate hours of rehearsal. His patience is untiring. A double-bass player will say: "This cannot be done this way," and then Casals will show that it can. He never has to shout to be obeyed and always he encourages. If something does not suit him—say a clarinet or an oboe phrase—he says to the player: "Good, very good, now let us do it again," and it would be "again" and "again," and "good, very good," until by virtue of his subtle way of making each player feel the ideas are his own, it does indeed become good—Casals in repetition singing out at the top of his voice, waving his arms (at times his whole body, as if he were playing every instrument in the orchestra) in demonstration of certain things he wants, and leaving no doubt in the minds of any of the players as to his musical ideas. This went on for weeks of intensive work, every spring and autumn; weeks of daily and nightly rehearsals with ten or more concerts given during each of the two seasons. The rehearsals were long hours of absorbed attention and unflagging work, with half an hour of relaxation in between when the men lighted pipes and cigars and sat around in groups, much of the time in eager discussion or controversy over some question of their previous hours of work, analyzing the piece in hand and studying its meaning.

Viewing the orchestra from its position as a real center of musical influence, and asking questions concerning its early days, one finds so much to interest and astonish, so much concerning the trials and struggles, the notable pioneer work, and the valiant championing of its sponsor and conductor under the most discouraging of circumstances, that it seems the story of the orchestra from its beginning should be told. Pablo Casals poured out unstinting service and sacrifice and devotion of the most fruitful nature, and the benefits wrought by him were shared by all, workingmen and leisure class alike.

Indeed, a unique feature of Casals' accomplishment in Barcelona is his introduction of music into the family life of the laboring classes. Realizing that in addition to its emotional side music has a moral function, in that it cannot remain selfish and must be shared, and working to present that social side in its very best manifestation, he made of musical experience—so often thought of as a luxury of the rich—a matter of bread and meat with hundreds of men and women in Barcelona. This, in his own heart, is one of Pablo Casals' greatest satisfactions.

For sixty or seventy years before the Pablo Casals Orchestra was founded, there had been other orchestras in Barcelona; not regularly established orchestras, but players brought together from the various theaters whenever occasion required. In early days Ferdinand Hiller, the German conductor and composer, had gone there to conduct the opera, and had given one movement of one symphony of Beethoven for the first time. In 1891, Nicolau had organized an association of concerts, and later Crickboom, the violinist of the Belgian quartet, had brought together and conducted

a new orchestra, but resigned after many years of effort. Enrique Granados, himself a Catalan, founded and conducted
a society of classical concerts and kept it going for two years,
then failed also. Lamotte de Grignon, conductor of the distinguished Municipal Band of Barcelona, had a symphony
orchestra for a number of years, and another society held a
string orchestra together for awhile, giving occasional concerts. Many other organizations were attempted but all eventually disappeared, owing to their not being established in
the right way. Orchestras could not endure, for it was not
possible to secure sufficient rehearsals, and moreover, conditions in Barcelona in those days were far from satisfactory for
successful cooperative administration.

Casals wanted to apply his interest and influence to the
improvement of the situation, and had not at first intended
to become the conductor himself. He went to the musicians
who had the already existing orchestras and talked over the
conditions with them. They agreed that these were not ideal
and that better means and methods were sadly needed; but
when asked whether they were prepared to do the work necessary to lift musical affairs to an altogether higher plane, they
said they were not, that the difficulties were really insurmountable. Casals had dreamed of creating a symphony orchestra of international importance; but they told him that
he had been away from the country too long and did not
know the real state of things, could not see the matter in its
true aspect or grasp how impossible it was to make such significant changes.

Casals felt that Barcelona was much too metropolitan a

city to be so behind the times in the matter of orchestral concerts. He now saw that there was only one thing to do: he would have to try to accomplish his purpose himself. He turned to the various friends who he knew would inspire him with confidence and give him sympathetic understanding, and made strenuous efforts to interest other people. Again and again he appealed to different prominent citizens for help in arranging for the new organization. But in vain. He met with more or less ridicule; to some it appeared like sheer madness, for he said he would need a large amount of money, and they could not understand his purpose, it seemed to them unnecessary; they had orchestras, why anything more? Even those who were friendly to his ideas thought it folly to persist under such circumstances.

So Casals was obliged to take further matters entirely into his own hands. He engaged men on his own responsibility, paid them himself, and began rehearsals. Every imaginable difficulty followed: he met with both professional and political antagonism; articles were printed against him, and one of Barcelona's most influential men, when approached for interest and understanding, refused both, saying that he cared for neither music nor bullfights!

The organizing work became more than Casals could cope with physically, and through anxiety, responsibility and discouragement he broke down nervously and became unable to work for many weeks. But he understood what would be the psychological effect of giving in at that time, and, sick as he was, he called a meeting of the men, went down to them and begged them to stick together as a body even if they did not rehearse; he would pay them just the same for as long a period as he was unable to be with them. (And the fact, interesting to learn and not easy to get Pablo Casals to confess to, is that the money he spent in the years before success came to put the organization on its own feet mounted well into six figures.) He explained that this was a crucial time. If they went to pieces then he could never get them together again. The men agreed to meet regularly. Sometimes they read things through, with Pablo's brother Enric directing, and other times they just gathered in the hall and sat there, waiting. Thus weeks passed.

A little later, a group of these men went to Casals when he lay ill, and said: "Maestro, what *shall* we do?" And he answered: "You must go to your rehearsal hall at the same time day after day and play, play, play." Naturally, this was difficult, and it was of great credit to them, as well as to Casals' power of personality, that the men stood so closely by him through everything.

In the meantime he had firm friends working for and with him. His close friend, Señor Capdevila, knew all his plans, was deeply interested and did much of the early thankless work for him, trying to make people understand the importance of what Casals wanted. He would meet with disappointment, but would go at it again and again. He formed a committee and acted as the first treasurer of the orchestra. As Casals puts it: "He passed through the martyrdom of it with me." His wife, Señora Capdevila, took upon herself the duties of secretary and gave endless hours of work, even doing correction of orchestra parts, which, in her busy life,

In the Plaza Pi Margall, Vendrell, 1927

Orquestra Pau Casals with Eugene Ysaye as soloist

meant working many times into the small hours of the morning. These people put their full hearts into the undertaking. Señor Capdevila later died, and his widow continued the loyal gift of service—to this day working in the orchestra's interests, never having taken compensation for any of the time she has spent.

With his return to health Casals seemed to have gained a new strength for his endeavors. One of the difficulties had been that politics played so large a part in Catalonian affairs. It was not easy, in Barcelona, to get parties of different political ideas to amalgamate. One thing that made Casals very happy was the fact that he was able to show that music was one meeting ground on which there need be no division. The two presidents—royalist and separatist—met in conference with him and the results were most felicitous.

No one had thought it possible that ideas such as those Casals so tenaciously clung to *could* be made to work out successfully, but in his own mind his course lay clear and never for a second did he falter. He knew his vision to be possible of achievement and with an almost fanatical spirit of artistic devotion he carried everything before him. A very great moral support came through Señor Vidal-Quadras, president of the orchestral society and one of Casals' earliest friends. It was in the fine old home of Vidal-Quadras, where amateur chamber music was regularly indulged in, that Pablo Casals had played for the first time in string quartet. This distinguished gentleman was a marvelous friend to the orchestra—his untiring enthusiasm communicating itself to everyone, his high social rank lending prestige to the move-

97

ment. He had said to Casals: "I must give you what little I can," then, as Casals says, "gave so much, in so noble and wonderful a way, that it meant everything."

The systematic training of the players had now begun in earnest and the consolidation of the orchestra took place. Concerts were given and subscriptions commenced coming in—growing gradually—and during the second season people began to say: "Casals? Wonderful after all! Not so crazy as we thought!"

The orchestra became a corporation and Señor Joaquin Pena, one of Casals' warmest personal friends and his first and stoutest supporter in the early work, was made secretary. Señor Pena, a man of great personality and idealism, and once very wealthy, had spent everything helping music in Catalonia, and particularly in Barcelona. Gifted as a writer, an inveterate reader in all languages, he has translated into Catalan everything that any musical organization there has wanted to perform: the chorus of Beethoven's Ninth Symphony, Haydn's *Creation*, Wagner's *Tristan*, the songs of Schubert and Schumann, Brahms and many other composers. He had the cause of the Pablo Casals Orchestra deeply at heart, and though more idealistic than optimistic (he knew too well the difficulties!) had genuine conviction on the subject and gave thoroughgoing and devoted support.

The antagonism and professional jealousy of the earlier days were now giving way to interest and even to tentative cooperation. Conductors and composers who had at first held aloof were not proof against Casals' own friendly attitude; he refused always to construe things unhelpfully and simply would not accept any unfriendliness. He offered to perform in his concerts compositions of the very men who had worked most powerfully against him at the start, and thus completely won them over. A spirit of new faith was taking hold; his men in the orchestra, showing a profound interest in their work, were devoted to him and there existed between players and leader a mutual regard and a relationship far beyond the ordinary. A constantly increasing number of music lovers were giving him intelligent interest and support.

His brother Enric,[1] a violinist, head of the Casals Institute of Music in Barcelona and concert master of the orchestra, had been what Pablo characterizes as "a pillar" of the orchestra from its inception; feeling for the whole matter the same deep conviction as his brother and saying to him: "Tell me what to do and I will do it," he gave a devotion that knew no limit. Early developing his qualifications as a leader, he soon won the respect of the orchestra and Pablo put more and more upon his shoulders the work of conducting rehearsals. He became assistant conductor and had his own share in the concert programs. By 1928 the orchestra was self-supporting. Its first concert took place on October 13, 1920. There were over one thousand subscribers and patrons, and the large hall holding four thousand people was always filled. Pablo Casals never accepted any salary for his labors.

The Catalan Palace of Music, in the auditorium of which

---

[1] Enric, who did not leave his country at the time of the Franco conquest, "was obliged," to quote Casals, "to remain in Barcelona in order to earn a living for his family." He was thus able to protect those things which were Pablo's, in the house in which he lived on the Diagonal, for it was Pablo's home too, when in Barcelona, and nothing of his there has been disturbed.

the concerts of the Pablo Casals Orchestra were held, is the home of the Orfeo Catalá, a choral organization founded in 1891, the director, Luis Millet y Pages, having exercised his leadership for more than thirty-five years. A musician of exceptional character and quality, with an intensity of artistic spirit and a red-hot enthusiasm, Millet infused his famous body of singers with a force and power that were felt the length and breadth of musical Spain. The students and members of the Society of the Orfeo Catalá were at work daily and all day, early in the morning and late at night, rehearsals and classes in choral work and in instrumental ensemble sometimes commencing as early as six in the morning.

Perhaps one reason why the people of Catalonia are able to work so efficiently, and are willing to meet the most exacting demands of a conductor for rehearsals, is that they have been used to continuous labor from childhood. Having always had to work intensively for any kind of satisfactory results in the cultivation of their soil, when their enthusiasm or interest is aroused, musically or otherwise—and Catalonians have the reputation of being among the most musical people in Spain—they gladly bring this same spirit of genuine effort to its service.

That is why one can find a body of young singers, such as the Orfeo Gracienc, another very fine Barcelona organization, ready to combine, as they did the year of the Schubert Centennial, with the Pablo Casals Orchestra in a performance of astonishing beauty and finish of the difficult Schubert Mass in E flat. This chorus of four hundred members (some of them children but six years of age, and most of them

youths and girls of sixteen to twenty, with a few more ma-
ture singers among the basses) produced an almost faultless
intonation and articulation. Their crescendos and diminuen-
dos were thrilling to hear, while their fugal bits were voiced
as clearly as if played by a string quartet—these children singing their Latin and their Schubert with an ease and familiar-
ity that seemed almost incredible. They had had months of
incessant work with their director, Ivan Balcells, for this
Mass, and seven or eight rehearsals with Pablo Casals. Other
undertakings of this chorus with the Casals Orchestra were
Beethoven's Ninth Symphony, the *Faust* symphony of Liszt,
Haydn's *Creation* and Beethoven's *Mount of Olives*.

The love of conducting has been nothing sudden with
Casals; he has always held the idea that conducting was his
real work in life. He says that as a child playing the organ in
the parish church of Vendrell, he felt the "irresistible need"
of leading the choir—he would tell the tenors to do this, the
sopranos that. And later when, with a wider outlook on life,
he had plumbed the depth of his serious art he realized that
his early passion was in truth an abiding one; that the orchestra could unquestionably be made the most completely
expressive instrument in giving employment to his own
powers of interpretation.

Strangely enough, from the beginning of his artistic career,
he felt that the cello did not give him his truest way of expressing himself—he says he never thought of the cello as
part of himself, and his ideal has never been that of a solo
virtuoso.

In this connection, an illuminating anecdote may be told

of an accident he met with in California when on his first
concert tour in America, of which mention has already been
made. Climbing Mt. Tamalpais one day, he had reached
the top and had started down the other side, when in a difficult moment of the descent a big rock suddenly became
loosened and started rolling down. It came so directly upon
him that he thought it was his last moment of life. He made
a mad movement to the right and escaped contact excepting
with his left hand, the rock passing over his first finger and
crushing it. He remembers that his only thought at that moment was: "Thank God, I shall never have to play the cello
again!"

He did his first real conducting when he was seventeen,
leading the orchestra in the rehearsals of Enrique Granados'
first opera (*Maria del Carmen*) in Barcelona. Later, for a
period of years, he used to lead a series of concerts in Paris
with the Lamoureux Orchestra, and he has also conducted
the Colonne Orchestra there. He gave an orchestral concert
of his own in New York City on April 7, 1922, conducting
the New York Symphony Orchestra, and in 1927 led the
Philharmonic Orchestra in Vienna during the Beethoven
festival.

Whenever on his concert tours with his cello there was
time, and it could be arranged for, he conducted one or more
orchestral concerts. This he did in Rome, Berlin, Prague,
Zurich, in Buenos Aires, Mexico and Havana. In this last
city he was engaged for three concerts by the Pro Arte Society, a rich and important organization then struggling hard
for existence. Its leader of that day invited Casals to conduct

these concerts in the hope of giving new impulse to the society. So successful was he that, when at the end they bestowed upon him the title of Honorary President and Conductor of the Havana Symphony Orchestra and he made a speech of thanks and then appealed to the audience for their assistance and their understanding of the importance of such a symphonic organization, an immediate and astonishing result was attained. One man called out "I will' give one thousand dollars!" and another, "five hundred dollars!" and so on in wildest enthusiasm. The men in the orchestra were greatly excited and Casals was embraced by everyone in turn!

In all these years of travel and solo playing, Pablo Casals had been thinking of his own country and had been "very dearly waiting" for the moment in which he could devote part of his activities to his home city. That moment came in due time and, as has been related, he now had this orchestra of his own well established in Barcelona. Orchestral work makes a deeper appeal to Casals than solo work, perhaps largely because of its human side; he thoroughly enjoys having to deal with a hundred or more men.

In the meantime he was asked everywhere as guest conductor. But he refused, for he was offered two or three rehearsals at best, and often less, and he says that without rehearsals it is impossible to do good work or to express himself musically. He was, however, for a long time one of the regular yearly conductors of the London Symphony Orchestra.

Of his appearance in London, December 1927, when in one week he was the conductor of the symphony and soloist of the Philharmonic Society, Fox-Strangways of the *London Observer* wrote:

> Whether with the bow or the stick, he plays as if he held a responsible trust, determined that at all costs the purity of the faith shall not suffer at his hands. He refrains from anything histrionic or ephemeral; he wants the truth of it. So the tempi of Beethoven's Seventh Symphony were what excitable people call "dry"; they do not realize how much they have destroyed Beethoven and Brahms for us by their fussy sentimentality, and that the only way to get these back is to mean every word of them, as he does. . . . In whatever he does he seems to aim at some invisible and unattainable ideal, and if some part of that is reached immediately to set the standard higher. . . . This scholar-artist is the most musical musician alive today.

Casals says that when he is conducting he has no preferences. He likes all of the works being played as far as they have a musical interest; the one he is conducting at the moment seems always to be the one he cares for most. In answer to various questions concerning conducting, Casals—who spoke of Arturo Toscanini and Wilhelm Furtwaengler without hesitation as the greatest conductors of our time—expressed himself as follows:

> A great conductor first of all must be a great interpreter. The main thing is to have a full and clear comprehension of the works to be performed; perfection

can only be reached with hard and constant labor. There should be many rehearsals, and the conductor should always have interesting things to say. I make the base of my programs that which is classic, but naturally do not refuse new ideas. Owing to the character of my orchestra, and the limited number of our concerts, we can play only those works of modern composers that have survived public censorship.¹ I enjoy the rehearsals even more than the conducting of the orchestra in public. The important thing is to communicate one's own sensations to the players, and to make one's ideals understandable. To know how to get in touch with others, to be able to convince one's men and impress one's own originality upon them, is in the highest degree a mark of capability in a leader.

In his repertory for the orchestral concerts in Barcelona each spring and autumn season, Casals had works of all the regular classic and modern writers of all styles and countries represented. But he made a point of including Spanish, and particularly Catalonian, composers frequently on his programs, among them Enrique Granados, Isaac Albéniz, Manuel de Falla, Juli Garreta, E. Morera, Joaquin Turina, Pujol, Toldra, Zamacois, Jaime Pahissa, Felipe Pedrell, Juan Manén, Lamotte de Grignon, Conrado del Campo, Enric Casals, Obradors Casademont and Luis Millet.

As the organization of his orchestra was gradually perfecting itself Casals began to plan how he could make concerts for workingmen possible. He had always given much thought to the class which seemed to be held from so many of the joys of life that richer people could have, and even during the time of his own greatest difficulties—those months of his painful struggle to hold together this thing he had worked so hard to create—he kept persistently to the idea of such concerts. When the moment arrived in which he felt he might talk of this matter, he went to his orchestra committee and broached the subject to them. But he received little encouragement. Later, however, through his insistence, a member of his committee came forward and said that he was in rather close touch with a certain group of young men who might be awakened to the interest of such a thing. Pablo said that the difficulty would be to find the right men, those who would be capable of exercising an influence on their fellow workers.

To the Polytechnic then one night this man took Casals. The Polytechnic is a night school for the laboring classes and here Casals met a number of men to whom he ventured to sketch his conception of a workingman's association for concerts, begging them to give the idea their most thoughtful consideration. Following this meeting by but a few days, six or seven of these workingmen came to talk with Casals concerning his proposition, came directly from work in their overalls and smocks and blouses. Pablo spoke freely of his hopes but found that there was a certain mistrust in the men's attitude. They did not know how to accept such overtures, for they were not accustomed to be recipients of anything they had not worked for. It took much discussing and argu-

ing on Casals' part to gain their full confidence, but eventually he made them feel that he was really their friend and
seeking their own good. In quick succession a number of
meetings followed in which tentative plans for the creation
of a workingman's musical association were established.

This first group of men began visiting the various trade
syndicates, talking with laborers in all the different fields of
work, and soon the outline of an experimental form of society
began to take shape in their minds. It was not easy to determine just what constituted the "workingman" class, just
what standard to judge by, and many tangles arose with fine
points to adjust. But it was all worked out to the general
satisfaction and in the final decision membership became a
matter of earning capacity: anyone with a wage of over five
hundred pesetas a month was to be refused admission—such
affluence would be altogether too demoralizing!

A trial concert was given in the Circus Olympic at very
low prices even before the association was thoroughly co-
ordinated or systematized. This concert was so surprisingly
successful that a first official announcement was immediately
made of the foundation by Pablo Casals of the Obrera Asso-
ciació de Concerts. Conditions of membership were published. The Orfeos, or singing societies of workingmen, were
to be given the preference in participation; there were fifty
or sixty of these choral unions in Barcelona, thanks to the
early efforts already mentioned of José Anselmo Clavé, and
eager men came in hundreds making application for membership. The association became a fact, and its first concert
was given to a crowded house. The group of men who had

originally met with Casals formed the first committee and one of them was chosen president.

In 1929 the association had a membership of over thirty-five hundred men, with several hundred women members as well. Each year the society was given six special Sunday-morning concerts of the Pablo Casals Orchestra, and tickets for the full season of Municipal Band Concerts and for a number of vocal and instrument recital programs, besides an occasional opera performance. The yearly dues were but six pesetas (a peseta being at that time about sixteen cents of our money). The concerts given by Casals' orchestra for this organization were always filled to overflowing (concerts not, alas, shared by those rich in this world's goods) and the audiences were unreservedly attentive; something electric seemed to pervade the very air, Casals giving of his highest and finest under such stimulus.

A significant process of education went on here, for fidelity to the ideals of Pablo Casals became a veritable religion with these people. Casals himself holds that this sharing of the joys of musical enthusiasm with one's fellow men may not only be an enrichment of the mind, lifting it above the facts and foibles of everyday sober reality, but may even prove at times the salvation of life itself.

Artists who came from various parts of the world to assist in these concerts were all filled with admiration and respect for the work accomplished, and many returned to their homelands fired with enthusiasm for a like work in their own laboring circles. In England an association was formed with that of Pablo Casals as its model.

Casals discovered so much intellect and intelligence among the men of the association that he suggested they should write their ideas about the music they heard and publish their essays in a review of their own. Their objection that they had no notion of how to express themselves on the subject he overrode, urging them just to write their impressions naturally. Wonderful things came from these first earnest efforts—results that astonished even Casals and surprised everyone else, including the writers themselves.

The Workingman's Association published a monthly magazine in the Catalan language, one issue of which contained articles entitled: "The Relation of Art and Ideas," "The Intolerance of Art," "Schubert, an Appreciation," "Beethoven and the Late Quartets," "Stravinsky and Rhythm" and "Poetry."

# V

## THE MAN

Pablo Casals is of medium stature and not very heavily built. Possessing an inherent quality of gravity, he is in repose somewhat severe looking, but his face is most expressive as he talks and his whole countenance lights up with a geniality that is singularly attractive when he smiles. He wears glasses, behind the crystals of which are eyes with a penetrating and intense look.

Simple and direct as he is, and punctiliously polite, there is a certain ceremoniousness in his way of meeting people, a characteristic reserve and reticence, combined, however, with a fine courtesy and much charm of manner. He has a great dignity of bearing and is scrupulously careful in matters of dress. Ordinarily kindly and considerate in his reception of strangers, he is nevertheless apt to become a bit refractory when confronted by newspapermen, for he dislikes anything approaching *réclame.*

He holds a passionate belief in the necessity of fair dealings, and the qualities of equity and tolerance are classed among his strongest moral principles. He has thought much on all subjects of interest and talks brilliantly, with a surprising command of the English language and its niceties. There is a complete absence of affectation in Casals, and despite the acclaim that has been his all his life, the meed of admiration, tribute and applause heaped upon him, he shows a native gratitude, a quite evidently sincere appreciation of any and every small thing done for him personally.

Poetical and practical at the same time, it is somewhat astonishing to find in the artist so clever an executive also. He has what may be termed a strategic ability for handling a case and putting things through, knows instinctively the right course to adopt; and once the soundness of his faith in a thing is proved, he works with a singleness of purpose and a perseverance that admit no failure.

Because of his well-known public spirit, capability and enthusiasm, he was in frequent demand for advice and assistance in carrying into effect projects for which he undertook responsibility with characteristic large-heartedness. This enthusiasm of his enters into everything he does, whether he is practicing Bach, illustrating something on the piano, trying to get tone out of the little old worn-out organ in the parish church of Vendrell, or directing an orchestra rehearsal. And notably does this quality shine through when he is working to make his beloved music a matter of concern to others, those others whose lives seem particularly to need relief from the dull and the commonplace, and to whom the ministrations of art can be so infinitely precious.

With the high-strung and passionate temperament of the artist Casals feels poignantly the sorrows that come into life. He has an air at times of one who has himself suffered much. Glimpses of a transmutation achieved by his spirit—of a sadness translated into work—illumine much that touches upon the character and the capacity of this great and simple man, who has shown such sincerity in life and such integrity in art.

Casals loves the old-time colorful customs of his fellow countrymen and meets eagerly every chance of participating in their *fiestas*. It may be a *sardana* festival as at San Salvador, where, in 1929, a musical program was given in which Casals took part as pianist. Dancing on the beach was indulged in both afternoon and night, Pablo taking the greatest joy in the small boys and girls—Enric Casals' children among them —who sang in the afternoon amusing little songs about "General Bun-Bun" and other hypothetical personages. On the second evening of this festival, when his brother Enric had composed a *sardana* on the theme of the children's song of the afternoon before and the *cobla* had played it, there was such unbridled delight on the part of the villagers that the composer was raised to the shoulders of his friends amid salvos of applause.

Or on Vendrell's Saint's day, which he never missed if he could help it, the *fiesta de Santa Ana*. For the festival of July 26, 1929, Casals played his cello at the end of the service in the church to a devotional band of listeners, and afterward, coming out into the Plaza which was thronged with townspeople, he was frantically applauded. The crowd moved aside to form a lane for him to pass to the Hotel de Ville, from the balcony of which he watched men and boys of the village form human towers, a marvelous acrobatic feat that has survived in Vendrell since earliest days and in the skill of which Casals revels. He shook hands enthusiastically with the boys who "towered" to the balcony in one of the performances.

This festival was an occasion of special significance: a new organ was dedicated in the parish church and an interesting and much-loved eighteenth-century angel on the steeple of the church, having been restored, was again brought to view. It had fallen into disrepair, one leg broken and one wing gone; while out of a crack in the steeple roof, from a seed which had germinated unseen, deposited there by some bird no doubt, had sprung an olive tree, unfruitful but silvery green. This tree had been a subject of greeting between the Vendrellians for a whole generation: "How goes the *rabel?*" was the question each day in good Catalan. Pablo Casals was determined that this famous landmark (the angel they all loved was a really fine old piece of work) should not be allowed to fall into complete ruin, but while he wanted personally to undertake the restoration of it, he was obliged to content himself with being only one of his fellow townsmen in filling a general subscription list. When the workmen, in removing the angel for repairs, had to cut down the *rabel* the village folk planned to make a baton for Pablo from one

of its branches; but he begged that he might have the plain
bare rod as it was, and hung the historic little staff on the
wall of his home in San Salvador to his own great delight
and happiness.

The restoration of the organ, however, he claimed as his
own special privilege, his father Carles, and he himself as a
boy, having played on it in the long-ago years. Filled with
dust and eaten by rats and moths, the little instrument, once
so fine, had not been heard in decades—except on one wonderful day when a pilgrim's enthusiasm for all that could be
learned of the early days of the genius of Vendrell stirred the
Maestro into trying to evoke the spirit of his childhood from
its wheezy old tubes. His beatific expression and smothered
exclamations of joy then showed that the old organ could
speak to him still. It now had renewed life, and on this occasion several distinguished organists participated in its public
dedication to service once more, besides the organist of the
church, who had been officiating for years on the small substitute reed organ. The organist of the Cathedral in Tarragona came to assist, and also Pablo's old friend and school-
mate (a one-time pupil of Carles Casals) Bienvenido Socios.

One of the strong qualities in Pablo's make-up is his faithfulness to his old friends and his faculty for retaining their
affections. The upholding and preserving of a comradeship
once his in full truth he counts as one of the big things in
life. To have seen him in Vendrell, an arm upon the shoulder
of his friend the village carpenter, Jaime Nin, and intercept
the look exchanged between them, and to know of the famous trio of boyhood friends, Bonaventura Dini, Bienvenido

Socios, and Pablo Casals, who still held their early warmth of friendship and comradeship in fact as well as in feeling, is to gain illumination on much that has made for the extraordinary personality of this man. Not only has he the devotion of his friends and the deep interest and respect of all who know him, but in Barcelona if the name Pablo Casals happens to be mentioned in their hearing even a taxi driver, a shopkeeper, or a hotel *portero* will give unmistakable evidence of their feeling of personal pride in him.

Though a Spaniard, Casals has not the habit of putting off to a convenient *mañana* tasks that may not be especially congenial to the moment at hand. In whatever he is doing, a concentrated attention and an unflagging interest remain to the end. He possesses much of the "unused original energy stored within the race" and it is hard to believe him the true descendant of those Spaniards whose delays have become so great a byword that Bacon was moved to say: "Let my death come from Spain, for then it will be long a-coming!" But in spite of the passionate energy that consumes him upon occasion, a certain calm and deliberate repose of mind is characteristic, and he can maintain a highly philosophic disregard of passing time when matters of reflection call for leisure-mindedness and tranquillity.

That he has both courage and independence has always been shown in endless and diverse ways. In Paris, in the days when the French were not sympathetic to Brahms' music, he put that composer's work on his programs constantly; and he it was, as has already been said, who first had the courage to play on a concert program one of the unaccompanied suites of Bach in its entirety, proving that these suites, so long neglected, could become of undying interest to music lovers and of immeasurable value to concert repertory.

When people referred to Mendelssohn as demoded, Casals would not hesitate to dwell on the beauty he saw in, and the respect he had for, his music; and whenever there were smiles or sneers for David Popper, he asserted that he would make use of Popper's pieces as long as he played cello, for no one ever wrote better for the instrument. He also voiced his appreciation of a certain "soul quality" in some of the music of Donizetti and Bellini. "It is not necessary, fortunately, to have Bach (or to *be* Bach) always; everybody shows different qualities, and why not take advantage of this and get pleasure from it? So many people today begin to decry or discredit Beethoven, Schubert, and Haydn, just to give greater importance to modern music; it is so wrong that it makes one laugh, and one can but be indifferent to the attitude for it has absolutely no importance whatever."

In his own compositions Casals is very much a modern spirit, both in feeling and in technique, though his style is for the most part classical. In his youthful days in Madrid, when time and studies were principally given over to theory and composition, he hoped some day to be free to write as he wanted, although he well knew it would have to be through his cello that his career be made. Among his compositions are works for string quartet, cello solo, cello and piano, violin and piano, songs, motets, and some large choral compositions, among the latter a *Miserere, La Visión de Fray Martin,* for chorus, solo organ and orchestra, and a recent oratorio, *La Crêche*.

He likes to classify the feelings he holds for musicians and composers. He called Schönberg an "enormous musician," though he does not think all his music great; and he admires Stravinsky but is not greatly moved by his music. (The *Sacre du Printemps* he cares for very much.) With the árt of all great masters it is the same; it is "possible to admire many of the works without liking or even approving of them." Hindemith, "a fine good companion," he finds a great composer. Delius he admires as "a man of true genius; abnormal, but great, more genuine than Hindemith, perhaps?" He thinks that among the Spanish composers Enrique Granados was the most genuine musician, the greatest poet—"like a wild flower." Though Granados studied a little in Paris he was almost entirely self-taught. Manuel de Falla had a more modern foundation and acquired a great and splendid technique in giving form to his ideas—"had vast knowledge and was a master"—but his musical feeling was not of the poetic quality of Granados. Albéniz, who was nearly forty when he began to study in Paris with d'Indy and Paul Dukas, though with little more musical training than Granados, was equipped like de Falla with a fine technical ability for shaping his ideas.

Casals considers that in general the younger generation has a more objective approach to music than those born and educated in the nineteenth century. He expressed regret that circumstances have prevented his knowing more of the music being written in America.

Among cellists he greatly admired Emanuel Feuermann, and deeply deplored his early death.

Gregor Piatigorski, whom he met as a very young man at Madame Mendelssohn's in London, he calls a "very important artist of great charm and with a splendid technique."

Casals' thoughts are ever on the alert and he keeps open all the inlets of his mind. He believes that the more one knows, the more one is bound to be plastic. He feels that in teaching one *has* to have a capacity for changing; he has always made many changes in his own working out of methods and means, and hopes that he may long continue to do so. He dislikes the very word "method"; questions the effectiveness of some of his earlier teaching ideas, says: "To show by playing the instrument is better." Interpretation, though, is a different matter. "There in not only one interpretation, like nature it changes always, but the base—the sense of it—remains. There has to be each time a fresh insight; one changes constantly without meaning or planning to: only a real artist can understand and do this. It must always give the impression that the listener is hearing it for the first time, and the artist himself must feel that too, or he grows stale."

With a reverent respect for tradition and an inborn understanding that penetrates deep into the very essence of a work, he expresses with special sensibility the thing he feels to be latent in the music—though inevitably he impresses the stamp of his own genius upon it!

His opinion of the average man is a high one. He maintains the point of view that talent is a normal thing, that ordinary people hold unguessed faculties and that the gift of expression ought to be encouraged. It puzzles him to know why musical expression, for instance, which for him is such a natural thing—"more profoundly necessary even than words, and having more material quality in expressing insuperable things"—should not lie within the power of more people. Why should it be more surprising than the power discovered in the physical forces of electricity or the radio? He does not attempt to define or explain genius—which to him "consists of three elements: character, talent, and culture"—whether it may be a thing inherited or a happy accident. He says only that "when you discover such things, you discover God."

Casals is by nature a reasonable being, senses quickly where allowance should be made for circumstances, and is ever ready to give credit where it is due. His obliging spirit and remarkable understanding seem to enable him to enter easily into the feeling of others. He seldom censures and is, in fact, more than generous with commendation and encouragement. A young foreigner, in one of Casals' Paris classes, had essayed a Beethoven sonata—the fourth in C major; he played it so atrociously and it was so evidently beyond his powers that the others in the class wondered what Casals *could* say to him. In their own minds they were heaping reproof upon the player for having chosen this difficult sonata, and they awaited with secret glee his discomfiture and downfall. When the youth had finished the first movement Casals said to him wholeheartedly: "Young man, I congratulate you—on your good taste in the music you have chosen to work at; would you like me to play these first few bars for you?" An inspiring lesson followed. This demonstration of Casals' point of view made the other students realize the mistake in their attitude; his earnestness and tactful encouragement had aroused their respect and understanding and quickened their receptive faculties. In speaking of certain child prodigies he said: "When very young they were remarkable; as lads pure in heart and spirit it was as if something had spoken through them, then—contact with the world changed them."

Casals often used to get a cramp in his bow thumb; at times it became so unbearable that he had to stop playing, even in the midst of some public performance. In thinking over the problem and realizing that writer's cramp was caused by too great pressure and closeness of the thumb to the other fingers, he invented a device—a piece of wood readily attachable to the bow—which served to keep the thumb separated from the rest of the hand. This he used only when severe cramp obliged him to; and he confesses to having been much concerned, and also much amused, to see certain young cellists, nursing their ambitions with more devotion than discretion and eager in emulation of their idol, making use of this bow attachment at all times, regardless of whether the fingers needed it or not, thus deriving no benefit whatever from it.

With a *savoir faire* that seldom fails him Casals has met many awkward situations. In public once, when a loose cuff bothered him, he simply stopped playing, removed the cuff with great deliberation, placed it on the floor beside him and began to play again without the slightest sign of embarrassment. Upon another occasion, having to play in a concert one afternoon almost immediately after his arrival in London, he suddenly discovered that he had brought no cutaway with him. Had it been in Spain or in Italy he could have worn his Prince Albert and no one would have noticed or cared about it, but in England formalities had to be observed, and there was no time to visit a tailor. He rapidly thought over the names of artist friends who might be of his own size, and recalling that Mischa Elman was in town, dashed in a taxi to St. John's Wood, where he was promptly and gladly fitted out by the obliging violinist.

Casals has smoked during a great many years of his life, sometimes to excess, and it is a familiar sight to see him, his pipe reposing on his lower lip, the fire out, still drawing upon the stem at intervals. In England at one time his doctor had urged him to give up smoking, and in that very week the London Symphony Orchestra, at the concert which marked the end of its season, formally presented to him a handsome case of the best English pipes procurable. Casals, greatly touched by the feeling shown for him that night, managed to cover his emotion and make everybody laugh by referring in a humorous fashion to the predicament in which he stood between his physician and his friends. To this day he enjoys telling this story and as he dwells sadly on his having been "forbidden forever to smoke," there will be a twinkle in his eye, for as he talks he puffs at one of the very English pipes of his story.

Through his entire life Casals has been in continuous touch with the finest and best in art, in personalities, and in liberal thought. His own ideas are broad, his tastes catholic; a man of the world, he possesses what may be called in the truest sense a thorough culture. Speaking many languages besides Castilian and his native Catalan he is equally at home in French, English, or Portuguese, and speaks fluently both Italian and German. As a raconteur he is famous, whatever language he may be using, and his unusually happy faculty for telling a good story has filled many a journey with interest for his traveling companions. His appreciation of the beautiful in a sister art is shown in his own collection of pictures, which, though not large, comprises several masterpieces of Spanish painting; and in these, from his large canvas of Zurbaran, of whose work he owns as fine an example as any in the Prado, to the modern primitive painting of Mompou, he used—in the days when he could enjoy his own home—to take great satisfaction. He possesses also fine works of Isobey, Joaquin Mir, Pasqual, Vilá, Casas and Cléas, besides a specially prized Zuloaga given to him many years ago by the artist himself.

Essentially modest despite the authority so legitimately his, he can still say with convincing candor that he despairs sometimes at how little he knows! There are times, even, when he seems to be unable to grasp the fact that the attribute of perfection in his work so well known to others is as confidently awaited by the musical world as it is familiar. Some years ago he was broadcasting in New York from WEAF in the Victor hour, and had spent a full hour or more of unbroken practice beforehand, preparing with his usual precision every single note and passage in the piece demanded of him, the E flat Nocturne of Chopin. A perfect performance took place; and the short cadenza-like phrase near the end, so especially precarious a passage for the cello (his own edition of it different from others, and even more difficult), was so scintillatingly brilliant that his friends listening were fairly carried out of themselves. He startled them all by jumping up the moment he had finished, actually leaping into the air in his joy and crying out in a tone of positive elation: "What *luck!*"

In 1927, at the fiesta given for Pablo Casals, Jaime Carner, one of Barcelona's leading advocates, a brilliant orator, made a speech in which he sketched a history of the forces that had conspired to make Casals what he is, really drawing a picture of Spain. Continuing with a discourse on the subject of Casals' career from childhood up, he paid moving tribute to the boy, the man, and the artist. Casals in his own speech of thanks remarked that there was of course no merit in his having been a natural product of his surroundings, that he owed everything to the place in which he was born, and to all the good circumstances of life. He talked about his parents, his mother's devotion, his father's teaching, and his other teachers; of his good friend, the Count of Morphy, and of the Queen Mother Maria Cristina (still living at that time) who had been so kind to him. All of these had helped in the building of his life, he said, "and if any one of them had not been, something would have been missing from me."

# VI

# THE CONSTRUCTIVE
# MUSICIAN

A FAMOUS musician once said that it would be most difficult to write of Pablo Casals, for everything he does appears so natural that there is nothing to say. In making acknowledgment to a task so hopeless, it may be affirmed that no endeavor to explain or expound the musicalness of Casals is here being made; what he represents in the world of art does not yield to definition. The effort to write something that might have a bearing on the various aspects of his musical and artistic activities, and on his individual habits of work, does not, to a shadow of a degree, mean an attempt to give a reason for his greatness, or to treat of the principles on which his technique is based as though they were set down as rules to be followed. Yet by talking with him, watching his approach to a problem, seeing how he practices, and how he puts his astonishing gifts of mind and fervor of spirit to the service of his general musical work, one glimpses something that may in a small measure make intelligible the atmosphere of truth which attaches itself to his art.

The significance of everything Casals does in music— whether as cellist, conductor, pianist, in chamber music or as soloist in concert performances which send his listeners away with a feeling of a high ideal attained and set the whole world of music on a higher plane—the uniqueness of him, in fact, remains something not to be conveyed by mere description. Berlioz and Schumann both said that the good interpreter equals in value the composer to whose work he is giving expression; but it is much more difficult to talk about the ways and means of an interpretive artist than those of any other exponent of the creative faculty. It would be a relatively simple thing to judge of a writer by his book, or of a painter by his picture. Pablo Casals is a secret; both charm and mystery lie in the fact that no one can say of him he does this, or he does that, for the next time he plays he may do the same thing in an entirely different way.

Perhaps his most amazing faculty is his ability to listen openly to himself. His aural perceptions are extraordinarily acute, and seem to provide him with a sharpened critical sense for tone so that he listens to his own playing with a detached awareness, rare even among artists, and never falls into the easy ways of technical habit or crystallizes on a theory. Though he may settle down to hours of work each day, and never has done one note without, to quote himself, "splitting it to the infinite," controlling it through the consciousness of that one note's relation to the next, his mind still remains fresh to receive the dictates of his own spirit.

Bruno Walter recalls an incident: [1] "Arriving for a last rehearsal of the Schumann concerto, which Casals was to play with him once in London, he heard Casals practicing in the greenroom. To his expressed regret that he should have come so early, Casals merely replied that that was quite all right and continued his playing. At the rehearsal he played the Schumann concerto 'with all his saintly seriousness and perfection.' Yet passing the Queen's Hall once more in the afternoon he again heard Casals playing and 'listened to his intensive practice for fully fifteen minutes.'"

Even in his technique he does not work on a system of fixed ideas. Never willing to sacrifice art to theory, he steeps himself in the purely musical meaning and value of a work and makes his technique fit what he has to express. Always in his own work he keeps the ability to change, just as in teaching, as we have already seen, he feels the need of elasticity in ideas.

Being in himself a reasonable person, he has a power of reason and a quality of reasonableness in his working out of ideas which make the ideas themselves more expressible, so to speak. This is perhaps in part why he is able to work a detail out to a point which becomes useful for pedagogic purposes without crushing the spirit of it; and is perhaps also responsible to some extent for his attitude of mind toward

[1] *Theme and Variations*, Knopf, 1946.

all musical and instrumental problems. He believes firmly in the relativity of everything; feels that in art as in life, in music as in the universe, all is interdependent. His own clear grasp on the natural values of phrasing and dynamics, of line and of form, the highly developed sense of proportion infused into every new manifestation of his art, imbues his playing with a stern and ascetic quality of beauty.

Casals himself says that he does as other artists, but that each one reaching the same end travels his own personal and particular road, and that the chief interest lies less in the actual than in the psychological differences of their ways. From his boyhood years, taking his first lessons in Barcelona, he was in a constant state of mental enquiry. The things he was told to do always came very easily to him, and though he had a great respect for his teacher he began even then to think how he could do more than was asked of him. He always held the idea that points at issue could be settled in more than one way, and, impatient to accomplish, many times invented problems for his own solving.

He had the habit of writing down on paper ideas and thoughts as they came to him, and each fresh experience presented itself as a new vision in his work—he applied everything seen, heard, and lived to his art, enriching both thought and ideas.

In later days when his career as a soloist was becoming an established fact and he was giving six or seven hours a day to his practicing, he used to take any new work he intended to play and read it first from the printed page without his instrument, then work at it on the piano, playing it over and over, hearing and weighing the possibilities of musical expression, and then again study it from the score alone until he felt he knew it well enough to start practicing. By the time he began to work at a new composition on the cello he practically knew it by heart. He has always been able to memorize very readily. His practice of starting the day with a reading of a Bach prelude or fugue on the piano he has carried into effect also in his study of the unaccompanied Bach suites. He will play one of these suites over and over on the piano, feeling out the musical significance of phrase and note and tone apart from the cello, detaching himself from the familiar in that way he has of keeping his receptive faculties clear and unprejudiced; and not until he is convinced in his own mind (for that moment at least!) of certain musical precisions, will he turn to his own instrument and work out the technical processes dictated by the music to be expressed.

Possessed of imagination, foresight, and a high degree of independence, Casals has maintained a questing attitude of mind in his work amid all circumstances, at the same time preserving continuity of principle and purpose. He has developed old laws of cello technique, uncovered new ones, and has achieved ascendancy for his standard in cello playing. His own powers of execution exemplify to perfection the possibilities of virtuosity without display. His working principles, which have helped to make possible an enlarged technical facility in cello playing and have contributed to a better general understanding of the means of musical expression, have evolved slowly, by a process of always seeking the best way of doing each thing. A colleague of Casals replied, when

Pablo Casals

*From the bust by Brenda Putnam*

Pablo Casals

*From the etching by Schmutzer*

asked whether he had not an exceptional hand which made it possible for him to employ curious fingerings: "Certainly not; he uses the fingering that is necessary to make the music what you feel it should be." Indeed, when one understands how his system of fingering is worked out to fit the musical purpose of each phrase, it seems so reasonable and so natural that one wonders why it was not thought of before—why the genesis of such a method was so long retarded.

In the middle of the eighteenth century, the French cellist, Jean Louis Duport, introduced many changes into cello playing and made such important steps forward with his instrument that Voltaire said to him: "You make me believe in miracles, for you create a nightingale out of an ox!" To Bernhard Romberg, who was at the height of his career but shortly after this time, cello technique owes a still greater debt. Romberg was the first to make constant employment of the higher registers of the cello and is said also to have introduced the use of the thumb position, features which added greatly to the importance of the instrument.

In the field of cello instruction, however, the fear of novelty seems to have lingered longer than in that of any other instrumental teaching. The cello was for so long thought of as principally an orchestral instrument that even the days which saw the evolution of violin methods left cello technique still to a large degree submerged in the prejudices of superannuated convention. Cello virtuosos there were, distinguished and world-renowned artists; nevertheless, the principles of fingering taught in their day left the ordinary student struggling with insurmountable difficulties in his efforts to master the big compositions in the literature of his instrument. The principles worked out by Casals have not only actually lightened the work for the left hand of the player but, eliminating to a substantial degree unintelligent and clumsy slides by the abolition of certain changes of position through the extension of the fingers, have made possible a cleaner technique and a consequently higher degree of enjoyment for the musical listener.

Diran Alexanian, former head of the cello department of the Ecole Normale de Musique in Paris and of late years established in the United States, put into written form some of the main points discussed by Pablo Casals in his lecture course on interpretation at the Ecole Normale in 1921. He compares the "morass of blind habits" and the ruts in cello playing which students ordinarily are unable to avoid, to the "luminous revelation" which became theirs with the exposition of Casals' ideas, so clear and full of wisdom. The underlying principles of Casals' musical thinking are so well expressed by Alexanian that quotations from his book will be here made at some length.[2] It was Alexanian's good fortune to have enjoyed a long and close intimacy with Pablo Casals. Though of quite opposite natures and temperaments, they used to talk together, hour after hour—"and loved it," says Casals, adding: "Alexanian can define the indefinable

[2] Diran Alexanian's *Technique of Violoncello Playing* (Mathot, Paris, 1922) analyzes the theory of cello playing based on the principles of Pablo Casals, who pronounced the book of "greatest documentary value" and wrote in the introduction: "I can declare that nowhere in it is there to be found a precept of which the application, sustained by artistic taste, would not contribute . . . to the building up of a technique in conformity with my own conception."

ind express the inexpressible—and express it *well*." Alexanian in turn tells of the many "cello days" the two spent together and of the great arguments that took place between them, discussions in which Casals' "eternal logic" stood forth in never failing evidence.

M. Alexanian writes:

Casals has revealed the very essence of the cello as no exponent of this instrument has been able to do before; he has become the standard for all comparisons. He has developed the sense of proportion, in other words, the interdependence of values, in expression. In his playing every note that is not a *forecast* is a *memory*; this magician forces you to anticipate what is coming in the same way that he makes you remember what is past. The impression which most of the great players produce upon us is strongest when we are actually listening to them and only lingers for a short while after; the effect produced by Casals is quite different. With Casals each detail has had attention, but the details are graded according to their importance, and he goes over the same ground a hundred times, strengthening one point or adding another, until his ideal formula has been reached. . . .

To my admiration for his innovating genius, for his baffling wizardry with the vocabulary of the instrument and with musical expression, has been added also a conviction of a practical order that becomes always deeper and deeper, namely, that Casals leaves nothing to chance. All that he does is desired, reasoned, selected from among the several procedures that would culminate in about the same results. It is perhaps this little word "about" that should arrest our attention. Casals possesses what he believes everyone should have—such control of even the least of his thoughts that he will permit no mere approximation of his aim. He goes for this aim itself, and until he has reached it, he remains the docile and sedulous follower of his reason.

The science of acoustics, of which his knowledge is profound and which dominates the physics of his playing, seems to him too cut and dried to provide in itself the final criterion in his studies of emotional effect. In the matter of intonation, for example, he cares nothing for the "comma" arbitrarily dictated by mathematical calculation as the set measure of separation of a given degree of a tonal scale from its enharmonic equivalent. He exacts low flats and high sharps. He is not content with sevenths or with leading-tones unless the harmonic attractions governing them have caused them to deviate from their mean position—in which they are inert—until they almost touch the point toward which they are tending. This is what Casals calls *la justesse expressive* (expressive intonation). And it is a thing no musician can ever forget once having realized the effect of it through hearing Casals. . . .

On the cello, in order to obtain this supersensitive intonation we must first abolish the equal chromatic interval. For the distance between the two tones constituting the extreme points of an interval depends directly upon the reciprocal sympathy or aversion between those tones. . . . From the purely artistic point of view no such thing as enharmony exists—a *b* double-flat is no more an *a* than the word "enormously" is synonymous with "excessively." . . . The natural scale of certain orchestral instruments, such as the English horn, the clarinet, the French horn, trumpets, etc., causes composers to use enharmonic changes in order to avoid complications in reading which some slight acoustic difference would not suffice to excuse, but here the richness of the orchestral palette compensates for the loss of esthetic purity bestowed by perfect intonation. . . .

There is a certain sanction given by the public to the player who spoils his intonation by failure to attend to the details of his digital mechanism, a sanction which springs from the relative quality of the emotions produced. Great successes . . . have been won by virtuosos who played, in relation to expressive intonation, absolutely false. The public, as little analytical of the intervals it perceives as the instrumentalist is of those he produces, *thinks* itself content with this substitute for acoustic accuracy and manifests its joy by noisy approbation of some quite external qualities. Nevertheless, *with this same public* the atmosphere of equilibrium established by true intonation (which I should like to qualify as "physiological") achieves an edification of another sort. Casals says that perfect intonation is one of the great factors in our auditory emotion, and that if we *simply played absolutely in tune* we would succeed better in expressing the nobility and purity of a work than we would—omitting this element entirely —through all the processes constituting "style," such as phrasing, accentuation, the ebb and flow of dynamic contrast, slides, vibrato, etc.

Most of us think we are playing true, yet how many of us accept without demur the inadmissible fingering shown below in Schumann's concerto:

instead of preferring to it the following fingering:

We constantly meet with chromatic arrangements of notes implying equal intervals and an evenly spaced disposition of the fingers. To play "expressively" the chromatic steps below, however, it is necessary, by reason of the attraction of the *c* for the *b* natural on the one hand, and of the *d* for the *c* sharp on the other, to place the fingers in two groups of two instead of in one evenly divided group of four:

The structure of the hand does not permit any considerable stretch between the second and third fingers in this particular position, except through prolonged effort. The tendon that unites these two fingers causes a bringing together of their tips, principally when the finger joints are bent to facilitate the striking of the string.

Therefore we are entirely at ease when we play on the A string this passage from the first Saint-Saëns Concerto:

but the same figure reproduced on the D string forces us to have recourse to the following fingering, as explained in Example 4:

This elementary principle, though the demonstration may seem childishly simple, is still the starting point of our control of true intonation. If first absorbed mentally and then made a muscular habit (it would at first upset routine and could not be applied without patient work) it will prove a key to the solution of many acoustic problems in connection with playing. . . .

An overwhelming majority of instrumentalists think of any step in the scale as always a fixed point, as it is on the piano. The following examples of *c* show how the position of the *c* is in each case determined by its harmonic tendency.

First, the tonic *c*, which is equivalent to tempered *c* so long as it is neither preceded nor followed by *b* natural (a very high leading-tone which in accordance with the laws of attraction would draw the *c* down toward itself—for the considerable deviation of the at-tract*ed* tone does not exclude the less apparent devia-tion of the attract*ing* tone):

Mean, as tonic

Secondly, a *c* which we will place high (almost *b* sharp) because, as leading-tone in the key of D flat, it tends upward toward its tonic:

High, as leading-tone

Thirdly, *c* which, as the dominant seventh in the key of G, is lowered through being attracted toward

the *b* natural, its normal resolution. This is almost a
*d* double-flat:

Low, as seventh

Now comes the question, what position to assign to
the *c* when, as a held note, its harmonic role changes.
For example:

Alternative

This case is subject to the good taste of the performer. If the two harmonies exert an equally strong
attraction, and provided the duration of each chord
warrants, the held *c* can be changed from high to low
with the change in harmony; or, one of the harmonies
may take priority and determine the level of the *c*
throughout. We must, above all, *perpetually control*
our means of perception, the sole object of this sort
of study being to *cultivate the consciousness of hearing*
rather than relying, too confidently and to their own
detriment, on our technical habits. . . .

It is indisputable that much must be left to the
style and musical tact of the individual in the building
up of the so-called intelligence of the fingers. . . . It
has often been said that the fingering of Casals was a

violinist's fingering and could not be used by anyone but himself. I believe it can be shown that this fingering is excellently cellistic, and also that cellists would definitely adopt it if they but analyzed the reasons underlying it. . . . Violinists, by reason of the smallness of the chromatic steps on their instrument, use the first and fourth fingers for the interval of the fourth, the first and third fingers forming the interval of a third. Now Casals frequently employs the fingering 1-3 for a minor third on one string, when the intermediate step requires a whole-tone stretch between the first and second fingers. For example:

Not considering the shifting of a finger where a half-tone occurs as a change of position for the hand, he prefers the effect of purity which the following fingerings give,

to that authorized by thoughtless routine even when the whole-tone shift does not seem called for by the melodic design:

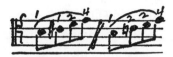

Thus, the result of Casals' respect for intonation on the one hand and for style on the other has led people mistakenly to think that because of some special conformation of hand he does certain fantastic things in imitation of violin technique. It does not occur to them to compare these fingerings with those which even the least experimental of cellists have themselves always employed when playing high up on the fingerboard, or that the stretch has always been used between the first and second fingers in places like the following:

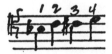

We are, therefore, far from violin fingering since the major third on one string is, with rare exceptions, always played by the first and fourth fingers.

The curious thing is that one readily admits an interval *greater* than a minor third between the first and third fingers, notably, the *augmented second* on one string, and the *diminished fourth* or *augmented sixth* on two adjacent strings, as follows:

Therefore, the following fingerings may be legitimately adopted in the name of true intonation, as well as in the cause of the least muscular effort:

This should the more firmly be insisted upon as it involves the utilization of the natural conformation of the hand. Mention has already been made of the tendon which, unless a special effort is made to counteract it, brings together the tips of the second and third fingers. Here is a natural disadvantage which can be turned into an advantage. Whenever there is no serious consideration to prevent, we must in our technique take account of anatomy. . . . Moreover, mechanism is not perfect until it comprises a useful cooperation between forces; waste of movement means fatigue which will be prejudicial to the whole of a performance. . . .

Returning to the statement already made, that the execution by the same finger of the two tones of an interval of a minor second is not equivalent to a change of hand position, I believe that if the following fingering at the beginning of the Haydn concerto is not rhythmically bad (as it agrees in meter with the breaking up of the 8/8 measure):

the fingering given below is preferable, as far as intonation is concerned, for it permits a reduction to the
minimum of the distance between the *d* and the *c*
sharp in one group and the *b* flat and *a* in the other:

Let us take this fact in thoroughly: that in the high
registers of the cello no interval of a minor second can
be achieved by two separate fingers, even thin ones,
when the rapidity of the melodic design precludes the
effective stopping of the strings or the displacement
of one finger by the other. If the procedure illustrated
above makes for pure intonation, notice also the
valuable aid it can give in the matter of style. Take for
example the first movement of the first sonata of
Beethoven:

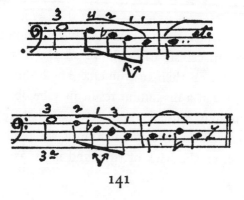

These two fingerings, cellistic though they may seem, nevertheless present the disadvantage of a perceptible movement of the hand and are therefore injurious to the unity of the musical line. Skillfully as one may succeed in softening the rhythmic shock or the shift of finger, both undesirable, is it not better to abandon entirely the useless effort they involve? Thus:

We all know that the harmonic octave of the open string may be continued by the bow alone far beyond the effective touch of the finger. This constitutes one of the most frequent and effective ways of avoiding undesirable slides, as in the following example from the A Major Sonata of Beethoven:

Except where there is some gouty condition or other stiffness, all cellists can achieve all the finger extensions useful on their instrument. These should be so practiced that a maximum result may be obtained by a minimum of muscular contraction. What frequently limits our efforts in this direction is the tendency we have to keep the back of the hand in an axis exactly parallel with the finger-board, for it has the effect of rapidly stiffening the hand and of spreading the cushions which connect the fingers at their roots in the hand without appreciably assisting the desired stretch. Furthermore, this kind of stretching forces the thumb to leave the neck of the cello, which robs us of an important element of security. In all the extensions, the thumb should remain opposite the second finger with the neck in between. In big stretches it is desirable that the first finger should be stretched back almost vertical and placed with the outer edge of its tip upon the string, thus forcing the lower edge of the hand further from the strings than the upper (or prolongation of the first finger). This obtained, the second, third and fourth fingers together should be arched obliquely in the direction opposite to that in which the first finger is pointing. I have never up to this time met a hand trained to the technique of the cello the structure of which prevented any useful stretch when made in this way.

Let us apply this theory. A stretch often necessary is that of a fourth on a single string, or of a major second or an octave on two adjacent strings:

It is natural that this position of the hand, besides having musical advantages—and even many more instrumental advantages—should not be easy to apply until our muscular and nervous reflexes have adopted it as they have the other positions. It is therefore necessary to work by means of little exercises, which anyone can improvise for his own use by varying the intervals played by the inner fingers, as in the following examples:

and so on, using different fingers and rhythms on different strings.

It is then that we can judge of the purity which the extension of the fingers of the left hand adds to the precision of our technique. Below is an example from the Schumann Concerto in which the extension of the fourth finger alone makes possible the one portamento which the musical phrase demands:

Here is another example, from the fourth sonata of Beethoven in C:

The abolition of all portamento in the cadence of this delicate phrase establishes an atmosphere of ethereal quality.

A similar fingering safeguards the elegance and unity of timbre in the Intermezzo from the concerto by Lalo:

Again, how gracious and flowing this bit from the concerto of Haydn becomes once the slides, usually looked upon as opportunities for cellistic effects, are eliminated:

When the distance between the fingers is so great that the stretch cannot be maintained without injuring the natural elasticity of the phrase (which is the case with the last three notes of the preceding example) it

145

is well to consider the position of the fingers in question as made up of two neighboring extensions, and to turn the plane of the hand lightly toward the last note of the second extension, giving it a rolling motion in which the finger common to both extensions (in this instance the second finger) acts as the pivot.

This same rolling movement is legitimately used wherever the stretch between second and fourth fingers exceeds the interval of a major second; in other words, in all double extensions connected by a common note as pivot. The following example is taken from the Bach Suite in E flat:

We have considered only those cases of extension where the position of the hand necessitates the use, in a downward stretch, of a finger lower than that which precedes the stretch, as:

or inversely, in an upward stretch, the use of a finger higher than that which precedes the stretch, as:

In the struggle, however, against unnecessary slides one may often have to draw the fingers together in such a manner that the distance between the first and the fourth is reduced to the interval of a major second, or even to that of a minor second.

An example visibly dependent upon this process is the following:

From the Prelude in E flat of Bach

It is thought of this kind upon esthetic and technical problems which constitutes the great and lasting contribution of Casals to cello history as well as to music in general. He makes it possible, as Alexanian says in conclusion, "through the material to *im*materialize technique," and in so doing "has established a complete code of instrumental logic which may be carried on and developed by every serious student of the cello."

147

Casals has experimented much with bow technique, working away from the habit of playing constantly with all the bow. He wanted, instead of adapting himself to the bow, to adapt the bow to his own needs, in the control of sonorities and intensities of tone, giving to each part of the bow its own peculiar power of expression. He has what practically amounts to a technique of the fingers on the bow, placing special value on the play of pressure between the first finger and thumb and the fourth finger and thumb. Through this control both strength and flexibility are attained, thereby facilitating the execution of all ordinary bow work and greatly increasing the possibilities of expression. In order to achieve the different varieties of tone color produced by changing from the use of the full hair of the bow upon the string to that of but a thin edge of hair, he permits the fingers to pull the stick somewhat on the thumb, making in effect a slight roll of the bow, without, however, loosening the pressure of the fingers on the stick.

His bowing is as logical as everything else he does. It has a structural quality which is especially evident when he plays Bach. One indication of his power in reconstructing phrases with his bow lies, for example, in the way in which, in the Bach C Major Suite, following out the idea given by the opening scale, he makes stand out certain scale progressions inherent in the later thematic groupings, ordinarily so discouragingly undiscoverable to the listener. He does not join notes and passages by accident or chance but bows so as to bring out to best advantage the distinct character of each voice. His playing of this C Major suite is clear and simple and yet at times sounds almost like a string quartet.

In the 3/8 fugal figure of the allegro which follows the Prelude of the Fifth Sonata of Bach, in C Minor—which Casals thinks the richest of them all, musically, and which is too seldom heard in public—he demonstrates his ability to achieve extraordinary diversity of tone color through his bowing. In the opening, which is *pianissimo*, he plays all the eighth-notes of the theme, with exception of the *a* flat and the *f*, but including the final *c*, *up-bow*. Later, when the theme recurs *forte*, he employs alternate up and down bows. Again, in the final exposition, *fortissimo*, he plays all the eighth-notes *down-bow* with great force. By this treatment he creates a remarkable effect of cumulative strength in the carrying on of the theme.

Monotony is impossible with Casals. One could give myriads of examples of his eloquence in treatment of Bach's counterpoint as well as in his playing of Haydn and Schumann, Boccherini and Beethoven.

In slow practice of a scale passage, without the bow, for strengthening the fingers, Casals exacts in ascending an actual vibration of the string through the energy of the stroke of the finger, and in descending a slight plucking of the string by each finger as it is lifted, with a pizzicato-like effect. By this practice the fingers are trained to contribute to clarity of tone.

He believes that greater or less speed in the drawing of the bow affects the pitch of a tone, and also that vibrato not thought out or controlled can be injurious to its purity. In speaking of intonation, he says that where sensitivity of finger in touching the string is quickly checked by a constantly alert sense of hearing, there springs a sudden life into the "vibration of intuneness." This is the foundation upon which alone it is possible to work out to their full value the effects of expressive intonation.

In playing a long crescendo note, as in the opening of the slow movement of the Boccherini concerto, he commences with an absolutely flat and expressionless tone, then at about the third or fourth beat begins to vibrate gradually, letting the tone grow and grow, until it glows with warmth —a crescendo in quality as well as in volume—producing an effect that is truly marvelous.

The gifts Casals possesses seem two-edged, but never inconsistent or contradictory. He holds a perfect balance between knowledge and feeling. Though he exercises the fullest functions of intellect and mind during hours of sustained and patient work, his playing becomes transfigured through the poetic quality of his own temperament, and the cultivated lover of music feels the inspired artist behind every note. So, too, a blend of two elements in rarest combination seems to lie at the very root of his musicianship—inspiration and control. In the building up of his great structural conceptions, *organized inspiration* might well be called the keystone of the arch of his achievement, compounded as it is of well-thought-out ideas, big lines and infinite detail; lines, definite, fluid, delicate; distinction manifest in every detail, and ideas translated into vital expression through tone–his tone being one of special clarity, richness, and nobility.

Duality is again evident in that he is both a classicist and a romantic; his classicism never dry, however, and his romanticism much more than any mere expression of sentiment. With his own great culture and fineness of perception as the force behind the flash of his imagination, he penetrates and subtly assimilates the originality or genius of each composer he interprets, and though employing the same vocabulary and the same rules of accent, he succeeds in revealing the emotional or intellectual content of each different style. Never does he sacrifice the significance of a phrase by making concession to sensation. The effect of his playing upon his listeners is one of exaltation and liberation of spirit.

# VII

## THE YEARS BETWEEN

IN THE EARLIER years of Pablo Casals' life, the steady flowering of the wonderful gift that was his—born, as he was, with no special advantages (except genius)—makes an exhilarating tale; and now, when he has established so many further contacts with the world by other qualities—his genius of living one might call it—the recounting of his consistent carrying out of high purposes seems of singular worth. His wide culture and a facility in languages which enables him to speak with fluency in English, French, German, Italian, and Portuguese, as well as in his native Spanish and Catalan, the strength of character and single-mindedness combined with the tenacity which reveals the Catalonian rather than the Andalusian, have conspired to earn for Pablo Casals the unique position he now holds in the eyes of the world. And, at the age of seventy-one, Casals' old magic as a player still works; the years of exile have not told on his superb mastery of his instrument. There is, on the contrary, something even greater than before in his playing.

In the period between 1929, when the first edition of this biography was brought to a close, and 1939, when Spain finally fell before the armed forces of the Nationalists, many things had happened to Pablo Casals, to Spain and to its people. In 1931, the Second Republic of Spain [1] had come into being without the firing of a shot and with not a drop of bloodshed, while at the same time, in Barcelona, Francisco Macía [2] proclaimed Catalonia a republic, with the right of self-government within the Iberian Federation. [3] Shortly afterward three ministers of the provisional government of the Spanish Republic were sent as delegates to Barcelona to negotiate with the members of the Catalan government. Autonomy was finally approved and established, but the Republic was set aside in favor of the traditional *Generalitat de Catalunya* (1932), which lasted until 1939. Although this represented a diminution of the liberty of plebiscite, it was accepted by the Catalonians as a compromise, with the hope, always, of later obtaining full satisfaction of their rights.

[1] The First Spanish Republic was proclaimed in 1873, and fell in 1874; its two presidents, Figueras and Pi Margall, were both Catalonians. The first president of the Second Republic (1931), Niceto Alcala Zamora, was succeeded in 1936 by Manuel Azaña.

[2] Francisco Macía was later elected president of the restored *Generalitat* and formed the first cabinet. After his sudden death, Christmas, 1932, Lluís Companys succeeded as president.

[3] The Basque country was granted its autonomy in 1936, when the civil war had already begun.

On the night of the announcement of the independence of Catalonia, Casals was conducting the Ninth Symphony before an audience of twenty thousand in the National Palace of Montjuic, and the President of the Republic was able to say that Catalonia saluted its return to freedom singing Beethoven's "Hymn to Joy."

Casals was happy in republican Spain; the governmental authorities were wholly comprehending and ready to do the best for the people. In Catalonia a remarkable movement took place. The administration of justice was reorganized; institutions of culture were formed to protect the artistic patrimony of the country; museums were installed in the new buildings left in Montjuic from the International Exposition of 1929. The university transformed its teaching, introducing the Catalan language. Hundreds of schools were opened, normal and secondary schools, schools of arts and letters, a workingman's university, councils of culture, and the Institute of Catalan Studies, while the Industrial University extended its teachings to all social classes. The intellectual and artistic life was intense. Casals belonged to various cultural and governmental committees in Barcelona to which he gave wholehearted cooperation. He was a member of the *Junta de Musica* formed within the Council of Culture of the *Generalitat*, bringing to it the fruit of his work and experience; among its first objectives were the organizing of musical education in the schools, the creation of a high school of music, the building of a national theater, subsidy of the symphony orchestra and the numerous singing societies of Catalonia, and the organ-

ization of important contests to stimulate Catalan composers.

A compatriot, Ventura Gassol, the Catalan poet, living
at this time in Lausanne, wrote: "I have seen his '*joie de
vivre*' during the epoch of the Republic. Those who have
not heard him address a concourse of his fellow men do not
thoroughly know Pau Casals. At the moment when others
have let themselves be carried away by the crowd, he—calm
and serene—would dominate them, talking always with
slow and rhythmic deliberation, both tranquilizing and controlling."

He met with the greatest consideration from all sides
at this time. Were they ambassadors or consuls, university
people, scholars, lawyers, or workingmen, all evinced the
desire to assist Casals in every way possible. Deep interest
was taken in everything that concerned him: he would be
met at stations, and automobiles were placed at his disposal.
He was frequently off on concert tours—twenty or twenty-
five concerts a month—to England, France, Belgium, Holland, Hungary, Rumania and other countries. In 1937 he
played in Argentina, Brazil and Uruguay; in 1938 he went
to Turkey, Greece and North Africa. He continued to be one
of the most outstanding figures in the world of music, al-
ternating his activities between his concerts and the work of
conducting his orchestra in Barcelona.

This orchestra, the founding of which has been described
in detail in Part I, had for many years been his constant
preoccupation. It was, in Casals' own words, "my obsession
—my golden dream—to institute a grand orchestra which

could take its place in the world of orchestras, and would live. The road to attain this just cannot be explained, it was something we all lived. But this need not deprive me of the joy of declaring very intimately that the orchestra did establish itself in very truth in the life of Barcelona. It is that which we all wanted and all hoped for and expected. Clearly there were difficulties—why deny it?—a dream like ours had necessarily to find obstacles in its way." Surely one might say that the orchestra *had* been established in the life of Barcelona, when a newspaper could report: "One afternoon last week work in all government offices halted. Loyalist officials from the president down through the ranks took two hours off to listen to Pablo Casals . . . playing Haydn and Dvořák concertos."

Casals is not of those who think of art as for privileged classes exclusively, and his was the first "people's orchestra" in the world, an extraordinary institution with a membership of 350,000—inclusive, that is, of affiliates in the industrial villages in the environs of Barcelona (in 1927, 3,500 members). The concerts were given not entirely gratuitously, but with a nominal charge for season tickets to workers, students, and their families and friends, thus fulfilling Casals' wish that nobody should be made to feel that the concerts were being accepted as a charity.

Through the orchestra Casals found the means of extending, beyond the limits of a soloist's repertoire, his own signal powers of interpretation, and he brought the message of great music within reach of everyone, rich or poor, who was willing to receive it. This was the gift which Casals had always wanted to make to his country, and his country accepted it with grateful and intelligent appreciation.

During the dictatorship of Primo de Rivera (1923-30) King Alfonso, probably advised by Primo, had made a speech in Barcelona, repeating words Philip V had used against Catalonia, which hurt the Catalans deeply. Casals, too, was personally hurt, and astounded, also; it was an abnormal thing for Alfonso to do, he who was usually so able and clever and quick. Hoping to regain the sympathy of the people of Catalonia, alienated by his earlier unfortunate speech, the king made the inauguration of the International Exposition in Barcelona in 1929 a pretext for installing himself and his court in the Catalan capital. "At that time," Casals said, "I had my series of concerts with my orchestra, and I thought he might care to hear the orchestra play, and in one of my visits to Alfonso I spoke to him of it. The king said he would like to hear one of my concerts, and a few days later I received word from Queen Victoria saying they would attend, and she asked that at the same concert I should play the cello. Though this was against the rules of these concerts, I naturally said 'with pleasure.'"

A special gala concert was organized by the Orquestra Pau Casals in the Lycée Theatre. The *sala* that night presented a dazzlingly brilliant scene, all the *noblesse* attending besides the usual public and a large number of the important people of Barcelona, and the first half of the concert proceeded normally. Toward the end of the intermission, the entrance into the theater of the king and queen and their followers was heralded. An express request of the king was communicated to Casals, that he should direct the playing of the Royal March, the Spanish National Hymn. Casals imperturbably responded: "It shall be directed by the first violinist of my orchestra." This response signified a veritable cataclysm: how explain to Their Majesties? Impossible: Supplications, prayers, lamentations, all were vain. Meantime the emissaries had to do their best to retard the entrance of the monarchs to their box. The intermission prolonged itself in an unheard-of manner; rumors and comments were bandied back and forth, growing as they circulated, and the feeling of the audience grew warm in defense of their beloved Pau in what they judged to be an impertinence of Alfonso XIII. At last there was nothing to do but respect the resolution taken by El Mestre.

The royal party entered their box and were rather coldly received; the Catalans did not forget and wanted to show their discontent. Casals was very nervous and, as soon as the monarchs were seated, continued conducting the program. Then followed his solos with orchestra. As he entered with his cello, an enormous roar went up from the audience, and practically all rose to their feet. It was like an electric spark. The ladies in the boxes were waving their handkerchiefs, and the applause was so long and so violent that the royal family stood also. Suddenly a loud voice in the theater called out: "*This* is our king!" And another: "If *that one* is king, our Pau is our emperor!" It was a manifestation against the king, though not prearranged. "It was scandalous, the police were in movement making arrests, a terrible thing, and I was sure I had lost the friendship of the royal family.

When I finished my playing the same thing was repeated for perhaps ten minutes—an offense to the king and a shocking embarrassment. I was in despair." In that moment Alfonso XIII must surely have seen his crown roll to the ground. At that time there was a censorship of the press and no account of what had happened at the concert was permitted; the papers simply mentioned that the royal family had attended. But the Catalonians well knew what had taken place.

One day, perhaps two months later, Casals received a letter from the king's secretary saying that King Victor Emanuel and the Court of Italy would make an official visit to Spain, and that Alfonso would be happy if on that occasion he would give a concert for them. "One can think how happy I was to receive this unexpected word, and I answered immediately accepting, giving up all concerts that interfered. The concert took place in Madrid in the Hall of Arms, which is of royal magnificence—only equaled by the one in Vienna. All the embassies, gala costumes, everywhere lighted candles, in the first row two royal families, kings and queens and princes of Spain and Italy. I played all my program and after that Alfonso arose, very impressively, and with him everybody else stood. He came to me and began to thank and compliment me, to be affectionate and concerned, and I saw that he wanted to rehabilitate himself with the Catalonians, wanting them to take note of his behavior. This ended, I tried to retire, but the king had not finished what he had to say. 'Now Pablo,' he continued, 'I must tell you how happy I am to have had the opportunity

of ascertaining how much the Catalan people love you'—
a great gesture, and good politics—'I wish the Catalans
could know my affection for Catalonia.' I did not know what
to answer—there was no answer."

When not working Casals lived a quiet life of study and
meditation in his home at San Salvador, riding his black
horse "Florian" on the hard sands of the Mediterranean
beach for his exercise, playing chess with his brother Lluís
for diversion, daily practicing his cello.

During the days before the forming of the Republic, he
had devoted great thought and energy to the rebuilding of
his home in San Salvador. From the well-constructed but
quite simple seaside house in which he lived in 1929, he built
up a most impressive *foyer catalan*, filled with art treasures
and surrounded by gardens, terraces, a pool, many fine trees,
shrubs and evergreen plantings, with a well-stocked farm
quite close by. To the original house he had added music
room, library, and various salons, one of which he kept as a
*"salle du sentiment"* with only souvenirs of his mother and
father in it. For another he had transported bodily the
decorated walls and ceiling, the crystal chandeliers, and
the furnishings from an eighteenth-century Catalan palace
belonging to the Count de Güell, an aristocrat of ancient
lineage from Vic. He also had erected a high sea wall, with
a broad walk on top, protected with railings, from which one
could gain a far-reaching view over the Mediterranean. The
whole place stands witness to the attributes of the Latin
in him. A high susceptibility to the influence of beauty had
full play there and it is truly magnificent. The effect of the

San Salvador, 1934

View of Prades, France

Casals with his brothers

Casals poses for young artists at Prades

whole, however, is thoroughly characteristic of his own good taste. During the work of building his home, he offered a prize, to be competed for by Spanish sculptors, for a statue of Apollo that should satisfy his own conception and fill the place selected at the foot of the sea wall facing the pool. The contest was won by the Catalan sculptor José Clará, who produced a work of exceptional strength and beauty.

Casals has not seen his home in all these years of exile. The Government took possession and used the place for at least a year, until after Casals had paid his fine of one million pesetas for not having presented himself to explain his attitude—"and," Casals adds, "for having collaborated in giving concerts to help the needy in Barcelona in the early days of Franco"; then home and farm were returned to the custody of his brother Lluís. Among his numerous treasures there was a copy, made specially for him in Vienna, of one of the few authentic portraits of Beethoven, one presented to the composer by the municipality of Vienna. Precious also, far beyond computation, is the tiny cello which his father Carles made for him from a gourd when Pablo was a child. He impatiently waits to see for himself how these things have fared during the troubled years.

And where, now, the bronze bust of Casals by Brenda Putnam? (All vestiges of Casals that could be wiped out were eliminated by Franco's orders). A replica of this bust exists, cast originally by order of Mr. Archer M. Huntington for the Hispanic Museum of New York, by whose kindly permission it was recast. This the cellists of the United

161

States, professional and amateur, united in purchasing and offering to Barcelona as a permanent symbol of their feeling toward Casals, in the year when it was learned that the city had paid particular tribute to him. On that occasion one of the wide streets in the newer section of the city was named with fitting ceremony "Avinguda Pau Casals"; he was proclaimed adopted son of the the city; a medal was conferred upon him by the mayor; and various rooms of the museum were opened for an exhibition of things pertaining to his art and his career. As the fourteenth annual festival of the International Society for Contemporary Music was taking place that spring in Barcelona, it seemed an opportune time to present the bust, and Dr. Carlton Sprague Smith, head of the music division of the New York Public Library, was entrusted with this mission. The bust was unveiled on April 25, 1936, in Casals' presence, at one of the meetings of this Society in the National Palace of Montjuic, before 10,000 people, a gathering which included representatives from all countries and at which three orchestras played, those of Casals, Arbos, and Perez Casas. Dr. Smith delivered his speech in Spanish, to the surprise and delight of his colleagues and the satisfaction of the vast assemblage. "The musicians of the United States," he said, "hope that this bust may be well received in the City of Barcelona, and that it may be a perennial reminder to the Spanish people that one of their sons—Pau Casals—occupies in the hearts of friends across the sea a similar place to that which his art and intelligence have justly conquered for him among his compatriots." The mayor of the city answered his address in

Catalan. The concert began about 10:30, the speech occurred at midnight, and the finish did not come until nearly 2 A.M.! Casals declared himself deeply touched and gratified. All cellists cooperating signed their names to the slips accompanying the contributions, and these were later handsomely bound in a small album and sent to him. Seven hundred cellists participated in this gift.

Shortly after the proclamation of Catalonian independence, an evening of homage—"Homenatge a Pau Casals" —took place in the Palacio Nacional, set in the exuberant gardens of Montjuic. Despite its capacity the palace could not hold all who wanted to be present to show their devotion to El Maestro. Assisting were members of the Government of Autonomous Catalonia and Representatives of the Government of the Spanish Republic, and at the end of the meeting the people, carried away by enthusiasm, obliged Casals to *tomar la palabra*. Pablo Casals, accustomed to express his sentiments only by means of his cello, did not feel sure how he could commence the discourse for which, with so much insistence and affection, they begged. Finally he began a simple tale of his own life and work, and at a certain moment of the oration, before all the republican authorities—republican *hasta la médula* (to the very marrow) as he himself expressed it—he said: "—and I who owe all that I am to the dead Queen Maria Cristina, who was my second mother." [4] The people at this point rose to their feet and overwhelmed him with thunderous applause. Why? Not only for his exemplary modesty, but also for his

[4] Maria Cristina had died in 1929.

163

civic courage. Others there were who had been prudently silent in the use of the queen's name. Casals, no; and this because he is an *hombre entero* (incorruptible man) and such men never fail to speak out the truth, even though it might be implied by silence.

The military insurrection leading to the civil war began July 17, 1936 in Morocco. On the nineteenth troops appeared in the streets of Barcelona, under the false impression given out by their leaders that government must make a stand against a Communist revolt. At that time Communists had no participation in the government of Catalonia nor in that of the Spanish Republic (they had not even a deputy in the Catalan Parliament). After a hard fight between the insurrectionists and the forces of the government police and the *Guardia Civil* of the Barcelona garrison, enthusiastically aided by the people, the movement was defeated in forty-eight hours, also throughout Catalonia. Popular indignation increased when this revolt against the Republic proved to have had assistance from foreign lands (Italy and Germany); the *incontrolados* (anarchists and extremists) in their turn caused destruction and havoc which cost the lives of many persons suspected (with reason or without) of fascism; despite the Government's efforts to dominate the situation, there was burning of churches and convents and persecution and killing of *religiosos*.

On the night of July 18, 1936, Casals was with his orchestra for the last time. It was the final rehearsal for the next day's concert in the Greek theater in Montjuic, which was to be given as a "Celebration for the Peace of the World."

Some people said the idea of the "Celebration" originated with and was organized by the Communists, but Casals, ignoring rumor, continued his preparation for the concert: his beloved orchestra was to play the Ninth Symphony of Beethoven. But when the day of the concert dawned, the attack on Barcelona had already begun. At this last late rehearsal of the night before, the symphony "was going marvelously well," the players seeming to sense the nearness of the end so that they put something special into it. As the Finale began and the chorus was about to sing, an emissary arrived to announce the suspension of the concert for the morrow, with the request of the Minister of Education that everyone leave the hall immediately as the fighting might begin at any minute. Casals said to the chorus and orchestra: "I have just received this message from the minister, and as I do not know when we shall meet again, I propose that we finish the symphony as an adieu and an au revoir for all of us. Everybody shouted: 'Yes, we will.' It was unforgettable, and the playing and the singing supreme." Today Casals' one thought is to lead his orchestra in the Ninth Symphony in Madrid, when the time comes that his country is freed from oppression. "I vowed that night that it should be my first offering upon my return." That epoch-making rehearsal over, Casals returned by car to San Salvador, arriving at his home at 1 A.M. Early next day the Barcelona fight began; the troops of Franco attacked from three different points, while in every few blocks two hundred or three hundred people awaited the attack, without arms. The *Guardia Civil* and the all-too-few armed soldiers of the Barcelona government came later, but Casals could only see the unarmed workers. In that first attack the Nationalists were beaten back in less than twenty-four hours, "the people's arms being only those they took from the dead soldiers as they fell."

In the midst of the fighting in Barcelona the *incontrolados* opened the doors of the prisons. "The criminals in that first period," Casals said, "robbed and raped and were terrible— the Anarchists following their doctrine, killing those whom they considered had exploited the people and were bad. The trouble is that the world in general attributed this madness to the supporters of the Republic." How many times Casals went to the *Generalitat* to protest, and the members said: "We are defenseless; we can do nothing; we have not the strength." As Casals reports it: " 'Why don't you leave?' I said. 'It would be worse,' was the answer; 'the symbol of Catalonian government would be gone.' In this dreadful turmoil our one wish was that someone should come and put an end to it; but Franco came, and has done worse than all. While the revolutionary people represented disorder at that time, the Nationalists *represented* order, but could not keep away from outrages and crime. And even now after these nine or ten years, oppression continues, with imprisonment and death a constant occurrence—while the flower of Spain is in exile."

The republican resistance lasted two and one-half years against Franco, Hitler, and Mussolini, and only Mexico sent arms, outside of the inadequate, old, and useless few bought from Russia, with payment demanded in gold. Mexico also sent food and—this was in the days of the liberal President Cárdenas—was the first country to give wholehearted welcome to the republican refugees. Many notable Spanish men of science, literature, medicine, law and music were offered posts with adequate salaries in the newly established "Casa de España en México," which when Avila Camacho became president was changed to "Colegio de México." The Mexican ambassador to France, when asked by Pétain why Mexico protected the Spanish refugees as she did, answered: "Because we belong to the same race and hold the same ideologies, and because among them is the elite of Spain, the salt of the nation, the spiritually superior."

Casals has expressed some dismay at the attitude of the great nations. "It is all very well to say that the people of Spain must settle their own problems, yet how can they do it when their enemy Franco has the arms? They must have some support, at least moral support. The Spaniards who supported the Allied cause during the war believed that the Allies, who were fighting for democracy and human rights, would help them when the Axis was defeated. Now we almost feel as if we had been betrayed. Democratic Spain received no encouragement, so it is now turning to Russia and listening to Radio Moscow, because that delivers the denunciation of Franco that the people wish to hear."

The day before Franco finally entered Barcelona in triumph, and when panic was mounting highest, Casals was hurried by his friends and officials of the University of Barcelona to the university in order that he might receive their honorary doctorate before he left. The document was made out by hand and affixed with the seal of the university —"this at a time when people were in despair and did not know where to turn; it was a deeply moving experience." Even during the civil war Casals continued to return to Barcelona from his European tours. He did this in 1937 and again in 1938, for one week each time, to give concerts in aid of the children, concerts that were held in hospitals and theaters, under bombardment, and with every possible difficulty to contend with. After the Nationalists occupied Spain, Casals could not get permission to continue his help to the children and old people there. He telegraphed the Mayor of Barcelona (a Franquista) that he wanted to go on with his work, asking if they would give him facilities for distributing relief since he was then in France and transportation was difficult. No answer came. Later he telegraphed the Governor of Barcelona, with the same result: silence. He was able to make certain enquiries and knew that the telegrams had been received. After that everything done for Spain had to be accomplished indirectly, some of it by underground work. Much assistance was given by the Quakers, of whom he spoke with deep admiration and gratitude, referring especially to the work of the noted English Quakeress, Miss Edith Pye, "who had 'terrific' personality, was a real general, and made even Churchill dance upon occasion!"

Casals would like to see a three-step program for restoring a constitutional regime in Spain. He himself is neither for monarchy nor for republic, but for justice and fairness to the Spanish people. He suggested as a first step that Franco should turn over government control to a provisional junta; the junta, in turn, would prepare the way for the re-establishment of the legitimate republican government, the last Spanish government to have been elected by the people. As a third step this government should call a plebiscite at which the Spanish people could manifest its choice between a republic and a monarchy. If it opted for the Republic, general elections would be held. If it favored the restoration of a monarchy, the Pretender, Don Juan would most likely be offered the throne.

Don Juan, third son of Alfonso XIII and heir presumptive to the Spanish throne, sought an interview with Casals in Switzerland. He wanted the opinion of an honest man and said he knew only two whom he could trust to be sincere: a Catalan priest (then exiled from Spain) and Casals. He told Casals that his life's dream was to give to the Spanish people that which *they* would wish; and that it would be stupid of him not to recognize that the world had changed—had gone to the left—and that he, Juan, would serve whichever the people chose, monarchy or republic. Casals says: "I was glad to have an opportunity to speak to him about these things, and to tell him my position, and that this would be his chance for approaching all the anti-Franquistas, and that many republicans would be only too glad to talk with him." Juan assured him very definitely that he would never return to Spain as king unless he should be called to do so as the result of a plebescite; to Vernon Bartlett of the London *News Chronicle* he had said most emphatically that he would not return to Spain in response to any request from General Franco. After this talk Casals intentionally spread word of what Don Juan had said, but since then Juan has spoken otherwise, claiming that the monarchy in Spain was the only legitimate thing. Another "deception" for Casals, who in his heart feels that a monarchy would not be a happy solution—might even lead again to revolution.

In telling of this interview, Casals added: "I have faith; faith sustains me— I wish for Catalonia and for Spain a government of tolerance and liberty. I hope and trust that Spain and Catalonia will know how to make themselves worthy of such a government."

# VIII

## PRADES

In may of 1939, when republican Spain fell, many members
of the republican government there, as well as of the
*Generalitat* of autonomous Catalonia, found asylum in
France, where thousands of republicans had also sought
shelter, Pablo Casals of the number. At sixty years of age
he had been forced to abandon his country, his beautiful
home at San Salvador, and his native town of Vendrell,
where, in the old church his father Carles had played the
organ and had given "Paulito" his first instruction in and
his love for music, and where many of his boyhood friends
still live. Casals was now an exile.

His first intention had been to establish himself in Paris,
and there he lived for a while; but he was very unhappy and
found it difficult to relate himself to life again. He became
ill, grew somewhat neurasthenic, and was obliged to lie in

bed for a month or more, unable to bear seeing the light, and lying in semi-obscurity much of the time. He stayed, as always, with Maurice Eisenberg, his pupil and dear friend, whose son Pablo is his godson, and for whom he built a cottage next to his own house in San Salvador; it was the devoted care of his host and hostess that restored him to health again. When one of his Catalonian friends told him about Prades, in the southern part of France—in the eastern Pyrenees, near Barcelona and full of Spanish legend—he decided to go there.

This little French town, Prades, completely surrounded by mountains, is one where Spanish and Catalan are much spoken. The Prades side of these mountains is French Catalonia, the other side Spanish Catalonia. There Casals is as near as possible to his homeland; but the Pyrenees themselves do not represent a more insurmountable wall to his enemy-held country than that erected by his own iron principles. The landscape around the town looks newly born, despite its age, so dressed is it in color—so fresh, so green and white and red—the houses on the hillside gleaming with whitewash, the roofs tiled in red, and all half hidden in the brilliant green of the trees. The village square—the "Plaza"—embellished with an old church, a bell tower of the twelfth century, and so-called "cloisters" Roman in style, finely decorated but, strangely enough, with shaft base and capital laid so close to the wall of the church that there is practically no passageway at all; a very curious effect. Near the church a picturesque old fountain is surrounded by enormous plane trees, at one time quite imposing, and the pride of the plaza; now, alas, sadly stricken in years.

Each summer a true Catalonian *sardana* (see pages 75–78) is danced in this plaza: anyone caring to be included in one of the many circles, large and small, dancing in all parts of the square (sometimes, even, one ring within another), simply breaks in and holds hands with the person on either side of him, without the slightest disturbance being noticeable in the rhythm of the dance. Onlookers stand at all corners of the streets that converge there, climb up on the sides of the fountain to watch, and fill the upper windows of the surrounding shops and cafés. In the summer of 1947, Casals acted as honorary president and one of the chief judges of the annual competition for prizes in this national dance of Catalonia.

Out beyond this plaza, on the way to the Villa Colette, the streets are also lined with plane trees—these, however, of great size and perfection. In the springtime there are numberless acacia trees with *bolas* of white flowers (looking for all the world, they say, like old-fashioned perukes or periwigs) which fill the air with their fragrance.

Prades lies at the foot of Canigou, the great mountain peak sung of by the Catalan priest and poet Jacinto Verdaguer. It is beloved by both French and Spanish, and the aura of legend and legendary romance hangs over all that delightful mountain country. The evening walks at the sunset hour out to the neighboring medieval monastery are particularly rewarding.

Casals loves to tell the story of Count Guifré (el Pilós),

the founder of one of the early Catalonian dynasties, born in Ria near Prades in the ninth century, whose body is buried on the slope of Canigou, when dying of a wound in battle, he dipped his fingers in the blood upon his breast and, drawing them down along his shield, said: "This must be our flag of Catalonia." Today's national flag is four red stripes on a background of yellow.

Nearly every inch of the fertile soil around Prades seems to be cultivated—planted in lines and angles fascinating to the eye, almost geometric in form—with vegetables and fruit trees of extraordinary variety and quality. The entire region on the route to Perpignan and beyond to the Mediterranean is given to grape-raising; vines, close-cropped and bent down with heavy clusters of fruit filling acres that stretch mile after mile almost without break. Wine-making is one of the few sources of income for the thrifty French in that Catalonian country between the mountains of the eastern Pyrenees, and the vines were surprisingly healthy looking too, even in this year of 1947, when other parts of France especially in Normandy, were in such need of replenishing their vine-stocks.

On the Route Nationale, opposite the Grand Hotel in Prades, is the Grand Café, where at almost any hour of summer or winter may be found one group or another of hardy weather-beaten countrymen of that region, talking (mostly Catalan), drinking, and playing cards; and one learns, with somewhat of surprise, that much wealth in francs is represented there, for the agricultural products of that rich valley, where the gathering of three crops a season is not an unusual thing, has brought great stimulus to the exportation of grain and fruits.

The change proved the right thing; Casals settled himself and his little group of Catalonian friends in a small hotel there, and began at once taking responsibility for the care of the Catalonian prisoners in the French concentration camps. He plunged into a whirlwind of giving, of gathering and of distributing, of weighing values and needs—"there was *much* need." The camps of Argèles, Revesaltes, Vernets (one of the worst) and Septfouds were those with which he was in closest touch, but there were perhaps twenty or more which he used to visit or keep contact with by correspondence. He was almost the only friend these prisoners had; he fed them, gave them clothes, and saw that they had medicines, and his own earnings were given practically in their entirety to this work of charity—"not a centavo went for me." He extended his generous hand to all whom he could reach. The camps were "unbelievable," "atrocious," "veritable infernos," not so much "from deliberately thought-out cruelty as from unpreparedness; everything was disorganized, and there was no food to speak of; the people suffered damnably."

Casals remained in the Prades Hotel for nearly four years, and eventually his room became an "office," efficiently organized, orderly, with piled-up stacks and stocks of things necessary to make life at all possible in these camps. He received contributions for this work from all parts of the world, including much generosity from friends in the United States.

In the camps certain groups were being exploited. Those mobilized as "labor squads" were literally slaves, and were paid but fifty French centimes a day (in war notes). Later, when more and more men were thrown into these camps by the Falangists and their Italian-German collaborators, Casals with his great prestige succeeded where others could not in securing nourishment for the hundreds of people (branded as "reds" by those who should have known better) who in those hours of anguish were dying of hunger and exhaustion. Food would come through in large trucks: rice, potatoes, and other things. Receipts would be signed—but often the prisoners had nothing to eat but rutabagas.

In June of 1940, while Casals was still living in the hotel in Prades, the Germans made a sudden advance toward the hitherto "unoccupied" southern zone, and there were rumors that Franco would probably push in from Spain— Casals and his little party would be squeezed between the two, with little likelihood of escape. So he burned all documents and papers containing information of life and doings in the concentration camps, and with great difficulty succeeded in getting two cars to drive to Bordeaux. It was at the time of the retirement of the Allied armies, and all along the way they found everything in disorder. They arrived at length in Bordeaux only to find that the boat they had expected to take across the channel to England had been bombed and sunk as they were driving through the night to reach it. A few hours in Bordeaux brought the realization that the situation there was a hopeless one for them and that they had no recourse but to return to Prades. The same cars took them back to the place where they had acquired some degree of foothold (or so they thought). Once more in Prades after the two long and wearisome journeys, they found the people of the hotel they had lived in for four years so frightened of what might happen to themselves that they refused entrance to Casals and his party. What next to do? It was an appalling situation. The man of the "Tabac" shop opposite the hotel heard the knockings and the altercations and came out to investigate. He immediately invited Casals in and offered what he had of shelter— no beds, but at least a roof over their heads for the rest of the night; and on the next day friends took them in until they could find a home elsewhere. This they were able to do in a short time in an apartment next door to the hotel, where for nearly two years they remained before they found the Villa Colette on the Route de Ria, about fifteen minutes' walk from the center of town. While they all could, and did, fit into this maisonette, there was little enough of genuine comfort for any of them; but there Casals continued to live under the simplest of conditions, and soon the place became a center of attraction for those Spanish intellectuals who, chased from their own country, found refuge in France.

# IX

# SEVENTIETH BIRTHDAY

FROM 1939 TO 1947, in France alone, Casals was the recipient of more than thirty honors. Many towns made him "honorary citizen"—Prades, Perpignan (when the mayor, announcing the liberation of France, at the same time proclaimed Pablo Casals *Citoyen d'honneur*), Foix, Béziers, and Montauban, home of the painter Ingres. Others presented him with their *Médaille de la ville*. Institutions conferred honorary membership upon him. Societies designated him honorary president. One could name places and honors ad infinitum: Montpellier Academy of Science and Letters, London Art Guild, Bach Gesellschaft, Catalonian "Associaciones," "Llars" (a home or hearth), and "Casals" (chateau or manor house), Paris National Association of Intellectuals, Beethoven groups, Expositions of Artists, and Fourth-Centenary-of-Cervantes celebration. Even a club of

Spanish bullfighters begged the honor of his associateship; one recalls that in 1899 Lamoureux had bestowed upon him, in Paris, the "Chevalier de l'Ordre du Violoncelle—*une foi et pour toujours!*"

The first part of this biography tells of the honors given him from young manhood on (see page 63); to them should be added honorary doctorates from Edinburgh in 1934, from the University of Barcelona in 1939, and from the University of Montpellier in 1946. After the latter occasion Casals visited the tomb of the French poet Frédéric Mistral,[1] in Maillane, playing an andante of Handel during the ceremonies there. Mistral had always held a very lively admiration and a great friendship for the young Spanish cellist, and this Casals never forgot. In 1937 the Cobbet gold medal came to him from the Worshipful Company of Musicians, that famous society incorporated by royal charter of king Edward IV in 1469.

On the day December 29, 1946, in Prades, France, the post and the telegraph offices were kept busy from early morning until late at night, and the ether waves vibrated incessantly: it was Pablo Casals' seventieth birthday, and the little village of Prades was the center of a world that day. Nearly every country had written and telegraphed messages and greetings, eulogies pouring forth in all languages. England, Scotland, France, the United States, Switzerland, Palestine, Austria, Holland, Belgium, Venezuela, Colombia, Ecuador, Mexico, Hungary, Rumania, Czechoslovakia, Lux-

[1] Frédéric Mistral (1830–1914), whose pastoral poem "Mireille" brought him national fame. His works elevated Provençal to the dignity of a literary language. In 1904 he was awarded the Nobel Prize for literature.

179

embourg, Russia, Argentina, Portugal, North Africa—all were heard from.

Some of the many telegrams were signed by six or ten or more. One from Moscow was signed by Miaskowski, Gliére, Prokofieff, Shostakovitch, Kachatourian and Kabalevsky. Musicians from England were represented: Ralph Vaughan Williams, Dame Myra Hess, Sir Arnold Bax, Elena Gerhardt, Constant Lambert, William Walton and scores of others. Word came from artists, writers, politicians, friends, from mayoralties, embassies, departmental committees, federations and secretariats of workers' unions, veterans of the Abraham Lincoln Brigade, New York, with signatures by scores on letters and documents.

The Mexican radio paid homage to Casals during various hours of this day, and over "Radio Mil," "Educación Universidad," "Metropolitana," "Cadena Radio Continental" many of his cello works were heard. Casals' friends there, headed by his Barcelona friend and colleague Baltazar Samper,[2] made manifest their realization of the spiritual values in the present-day life of Casals, believing in the high role these values had to play in the construction of a better world, and saluting "the illustrious artist whose career appeared so singularly illuminated by the highest of human virtues."

It was a world-wide celebration, and Casals was deeply touched.

[2] Baltazar Samper, composer and conductor, now in charge of research in Mexican folklore music and of the organization of the archives of this material in the Instituto Nacional de Bellas Artes of Mexico City, was in 1945 awarded the "Ariel" prize for his music for the film "La Barraca" of Vicente Blasco Ibañez.

Huge posters in Prades announced the French government's promotion of Casals to Grand Officier de la Légion
d'honneur, fourth and highest rank of the Legion. M.
Georges Bidault, writing on November 12, 1946, to thank
the President of the Provisional Government in Paris for
his personal testimony in favor of the promotion of Maître
Pablo Casals, had added: "*Cet artiste, je le sais, joint à son
génie de la musique la générosité du coeur et la force du
caractère. Il est un musicien de notre temps et j'ai le plaisir
de vous dire que j'ai bien volontiers signé son décret de promotion.*"

On December 29 Sir Adrian Boult delivered the following
broadcast from London in celebration of the event:

It is with great pride and pleasure that I undertake
tonight the delightful task of sending the congratula-
tions of many thousands of musicians and music
lovers in this country to Mestre Pau Casals on the
occasion of his seventieth birthday. It must be more
than twenty-five years since a timid young local musician was invited to conduct a Philharmonic concert
in Liverpool at which the great Casals was to play the
Schumann Concerto, and he still looks back on that
rehearsal and performance as one of the finest lessons
he ever had. However that may be, a prominent busi-
nessman who attended the rehearsal was heard to say
that "Young Boult can't really be much good because
he lets Casals do all the talking at the rehearsal." As
a matter of fact young Boult soon afterwards was

able to have the privilege of hearing Mr. Casals doing a great deal more talking, for he went to Barcelona and attended for a month the rehearsals of the "Orquestra Pau Casals" in a very wide repertoire, and it was a great experience to follow the wonderful lessons in style which were given every day, and to see the devotion of the orchestra to its master. During that season an enormously wide repertoire of music was covered.

I remember vividly one of the finest performa.ices of the Schubert C Major Symphony that I have ever heard, and then Saint-Saëns' "Omphales' Spinning Wheel," which had all possible lightness and great beauty as well. There was some Beethoven, and some Wagner, and even a Rumanian Rhapsody of Enesco, all of which were worked out by the orchestra and conducted with the greatest care and wonderful attention to the style of the piece in hand.

Since that time it has often been my privilege to conduct for Mr. Casals. It has always been a wonderful lesson and a revelation in the understanding of music. I like specially to think of several performances of the Elgar Cello Concerto, which I heard one observer say had the effect of taking the work out of the category of well-known and well-loved British works and putting it on the map as a great international classic. It was exactly this that we all felt as we worked it out with our soloist. We have had the privilege of recording it with him, and also part of the Haydn, and we look forward very much to finishing that with him in the near future, in fact as soon as he is able to come to England again.

He has conducted the B.B.C. Orchestra on many occasions and has always infused it with a wonderful insight into the composer's mind. He has been honored by two of our most respected British societies, who in doing this have greatly honored themselves. The Royal Philharmonic Society gave him its gold medal in 1912, and the Worshipful Company of Musicians awarded him the Cobbett Gold Medal for distinguished services to chamber music in 1937.

Mestre, we send you our warmest greetings. We hope that we shall soon again welcome you here. We thank you for the countless experiences of wonderful performances, and in particular we recognize how you have taken our own concertos by Elgar and Tovey, and by your performances have shown us their greatness.

Here we are in the studio, a large number of your London friends including fifty cellists, many of them famous names in English musical life, assembled to play you a short program under the direction of our old friend John Barbirolli. How we wish we could see you with us in the studio here. But we know you are with us in spirit, and so let us now listen to the music which will carry our thoughts to you on this great and happy day.

The fifty cellists led by Barbirolli, himself once a pupil of Casals, played the *Sardana* written by Casals for eight cellos (divided at times into sixteen parts), which has been performed on many other occasions as well: in Belgium, in various parts of France, in Zurich,—when he himself conducted an orchestra of seventy cellists drawn from all parts of Switzerland, before a large and enthusiastic audience— in London, at Herbert Wayland's cello school, where one hundred cellists participated.

Roberto Gerhard, well-known Catalan composer and one-time student of Schönberg, now living in Cambridge, England, also spoke over the radio, saying in part:

It was in the hour of adversity that Pablo Casals' greatness both as an artist and as a man were to be revealed as truly one. His untiring devotion, selflessness and true goodness of heart have given comfort to thousands of his fellow expatriates, and if there is a man today we can look upon as symbolic of both the plight of the Catalan nation at the present time and our hopes for its future, that man is Casals. Catalonia, as it slowly begins to be known, is Spain with a difference, indeed with a great many differences. The central spark of Hispanic incandescence is there, but, surrounded as it were, by a softer luminosity, very distinct from the typical Spanish glare.

There is a Catalan word that, significantly enough, has no equivalent at all in the Castilian (or Spanish) language, the word "seny." It is not exactly "wisdom," not "common sense," but in its fullest psychological meaning the inclination to take an eminently "sensible" view of affairs. Casals' art is instinct with that quality; I believe it is the one which has always preserved his art from the dangers of self-willed effects, or from what Paul Valéry has called *"les écarts personnels."*

Indeed when I listen to the calm utterance of a Catalan peasant or look at his way of tilling the land, with an economy and loving care that reveals an almost disinterested sense of beauty, or when I behold the fine architectural simplicity of the most humble dwelling of the Catalan peasant or fisherman, I feel acutely conscious of the underlying identity between the human attitude disclosed in these things and that which one can observe in Pablo Casals' approach, let us say, to the technique of his instrument, or to his rendering of one of Bach's unaccompanied suites. To view this fundamental disposition common to a particular breed of men, lifted by the power of genius into a sphere of universality, is surely something any nation may justifiably do with pride.

Casals expressed his gratitude to the people of England through a letter to the editor of the *Times*:

SIR—Ever since my youth when, at my first concert in Britain (1899), I had the honor of playing before Queen Victoria, I have received many touching proofs of appreciation from the British public. I count them among the most precious rewards of my whole life as an artist. Now, on the occasion of my seventieth birthday, the tokens of affection from all quarters of your country that have reached me in my exile are so numerous that I have to ask the hospitality of the *Times* for the expression of my deepest gratitude to all.

The life of an artist is inseparable from his ideals, and I trust that conditions will soon make it possible for me to come and express personally all the affection I feel for the British people.

A fellow Spaniard, Mario Aguilar, wrote on the occasion of the birthday celebration: "Seventy years now, Pablo Casals. When he dies we will bury him, not in the Escorial, for it has been profaned by the Falangistas, but in the Monastery of Poblet, where lie the tombs of the kings of Catalonia."

And they call him San Pablo de Prades, "pure incarnation of the Catalan soul."

# X

## CASALS TODAY

AUGUST 10, 1947—France—after a quick crossing of the Atlantic from New York to Paris—a night train south to Perpignan—and Prades, August 11, just before the noon hour. Then that same evening at sundown, at the foot of the great mountain of Canigou, the Villa Colette with Pablo Casals. It seemed unreal at first, when, filled with nervous excitement, we opened that gate on the Route de Ria and walked the length of the path lined on both sides with espaliered pears in full fruit and saw ahead of us an unforgettable picture: El Maestro in the garden, a reposeful figure, pipe in mouth, sitting on a high platform while two young sculptors, a Catalonian señorita and a good-looking youth from Switzerland, worked earnestly on their models of his head. Their working time for that evening ended with our arrival, as happened at each successive interview throughout the month spent there. A trip up one flight of outside stairs and we were piloted by Casals into his little room under the eaves of the red-tiled roof.

After nearly nineteen years Casals looks unchanged excepting that he has grown heavier; his face is as round and wrinkleless as ever, his color as fresh and his manner as alert and vigorous, with the same old illuminating smile. In this room the first thing apparent was the cello, his companion of forty years, his "alter ego," as he calls it, reposing on the bed, ready for the extra bit of practice for which he jealously reserves time every day despite all obstacles. He is relentless with himself in his obedience to the laws of his own convictions and those of his art. As we learned afterward, he would often play up there late in the evening, and it would then not be at all unusual to see a group of people, young and old, gathered outside the gate waiting in the eager hope of hearing El Maestro play, and listening hungrily to the music that came from the room above.

He spoke of himself, of his life these days in the one room of the tiny house, and of his few possessions. He started putting money in the Bank of France in years gone by, and has lived on that until now, when he is accepting pupils in Prades because of the necessity of earning. It is well known, however, that he constantly gives lessons without remuneration. "I am poor now, but I feel rich in the possession of many rare things," and he pointed to his cabinet bulging with folios, all in apple-pie order: to his cello, to family photographs pinned on the wall, to his books—Seneca, Fabre, Maeterlinck, Dante, Cervantes, Montaigne. He showed with pride a few bars of Beethoven's Ninth Symphony in manuscript, a recent gift from his friend H. C. Bodmer of Zurich, the famous collector of Beethoven manuscripts. Also the manuscript of Brahms' quartet, Op. 67, in B flat, with original corrections, pages glued together, etc., given him by Dr. Wilhelm Kux, former president of *The Gesellschaft der Musik Freunde* in Vienna; and a highly treasured photograph of the original Joachim Quartet, with the signatures of Joachim, Wirt, de Ahna, and Haussman. He particularly values three photographs of his deeply admired friend, the late Donald Tovey; a charming sketch in color, done in youth, at the time when Brahms said that he could discuss music with this person and that but not with this lad who knew so incomparably more; a truly beautiful profile taken in his prime, and a third taken just before his death at sixty-seven. It was Tovey who, as Reid Professor of Music at the University of Edinburgh, induced Casals to go to Scotland in 1934 to receive an honorary doctorate, together with Albert Schweitzer and Julius Roentgen.

He brought out an album of paintings and sketches, many of genuine worth, by prisoners of war in the various camps in which he was interested, together with piles of personal papers, letters, telegrams, cards, and articles received on his seventieth birthday, and numerous documents concerning the honors that have been bestowed on him in all countries. The postman in Prades says that Pablo Casals receives more letters than anyone in town—more letters even than the subprefect! The answering of his correspondence is work he cannot leave for *mañana*. He is constantly asked for help or counsel and considers it a duty to reply as soon as possible, and though friends tell him not to take the task so much to heart, he pays no attention and continues to dedicate time daily to answering the letters.

He told how during the German occupation the household had been constantly watched by the Gestapo and by the French militia, Señor Alavedra, the Catalan poet, who with his wife and children were part of the household, having to present himself every week to the authorities. They had very cold winters, with little or no coal, and many times not enough to eat; during one long winter, beans and turnips were the staple of practically every day's supply, and once when Casals fell ill there were no medicines to be had. It was an almost intolerable situation, but each year spring did come, crops reappeared and, above all, their courage endured until the occupation was at last ended. In answer to some of the many questions asked him he said: "I had difficulties more or less like anyone else, but, thinking of what others had to suffer, I found it easy to face. Dangers, yes, like everyone living in an occupied country, with the threat of the Gestapo always over our heads. They suspected me of being the chief of the Maquis in the district, supplying arms; I had them searching my house, but luckily nothing more. I have been persecuted as being 'a Red, a Separatist, a Marxist, a Freemason.' I am none of these things."

Before the occupation he had given many concerts in South America—four memorable ones in the Teatro Colon, Buenos Aires—North Africa and in all parts of Europe excepting Italy and Germany. Although he stood apart from politics his spirit had early rebelled against the injustice of the totalitarianism that was spreading across the continent, and this man, who by his art had become a citizen of the world, of his own free will had created spiritual frontiers which he did not intend crossing despite all inducements or flattery. Hitler's Germany first, and Mussolini's Italy later, both found themselves deprived of Casals' contribution to art. "I did not wish to put foot in those countries," he said. "When the Nazis expelled Bruno Walter I promised myself not to play any more in Germany until full artistic freedom was re-established in that country."

Casals was among the first of the anticollaborators, not through obligatory patriotism or because of political imperatives, but because he believed collaboration to be filled with injustice and ugliness and "not to be tolerated." "Numberless Spanish intellectuals and artists are in exile as a result of the suppression of freedom of thought, this affecting the whole of Spain. In addition as a Catalan I resent deeply the banning of the use of our own language, and the suppression of our art and culture."

Many towns in Catalonia had named streets for Casals, but when Franco came these were all removed and replaced by names of war generals. So also were the fine old historical names—Grecian, Corsican, and Provençal: "One of the ugliest manifestations of man this destruction of the history of Catalonia."

The unavoidable break of association with those fellow artists who, having in France's days of great trial collaborated with Vichy—some through sincere conviction, others as an expedient—brought him much personal sorrow.

Life in this time of occupation had always the feeling of great insecurity. A short time after the last visit of the Gestapo, Casals was writing in his upstairs room when on looking out of his window he saw a large automobile stop at the villa gate. An official-looking German alighted, then another and another, and he thought: Now I am done; the Germans are visiting me for a purpose, surely! His friends had already gone forward from the room below, and fearing that they would say he was not there, he called loudly from above: "Let them come up!" "Three huge men they seemed in that small room of mine, all young men. I received them at my door, and they made their characteristic salute—sharp and quick, and the first words spoken by their leader were: 'At this moment we are not enemy Germans, we are your admirers.' 'What is the object of your visit?' I asked. 'We have known that you were here,' they replied, 'and we wanted to have the honor of presenting ourselves.' " How curious this amiability, thought Casals, who had rather that these men treated him brutally than with "this horrid sweetness." He remained very serious, no smiles (they in contrast were all smirks and unction). He could not exactly believe what they said; some ulterior motive must be behind it all. Then they said that all the German officials in Perpignan had wanted to come and see him, but they had kept them from coming so as not to be "making a scene" for Pablo Casals, and they began telling how their fathers and grandfathers had spoken often of him and his great art ("music was so dear to them!") and that in Ger-

many he was a legendary figure. "Well, they wanted not only
to see me, but to know that I had everything I needed; and
they began to ask me (like a good mama) if I had enough
coal. We had no heat, and very little to eat, but I told them
that I had everything and was not in need in any way. They
kept saying 'good' 'all right,' but my attitude with them was
still most serious. 'Why don't you go to Spain?' they asked,
and I thought: This is the beginning, and answered: 'Because
Franco and his regime are things that I cannot approve for
my country; Franco is a brutal man, and if I would go there
I surely would be shot because I wouldn't accept things as
they are; I would talk, and in Spain today no one can talk
without permission or prison.' 'But,' said they, 'Franco is a
man of honor,' and I returned: 'This is your interpretation,
not mine.' Then from them: 'We are now going to ask you
something we hope very much you will accept'—naturally I
knew then that this was the purpose of their visit—'an invitation to come to Germany—Hitler and all our country would
like you to come and play.' (The Nazis had discovered that
Casals was a propaganda figure too important to be ignored.)
At once I replied no, rather unamiably. The commander
said: 'And why not?' and I said: 'For the same reasons that I
don't go to Spain.' They glanced at each other, and in that
moment I felt some danger, because their looks became men-
acing, but the commander spoke again after the first bad moment, and said: 'We assure you that you are wrong,' and they
made a panegyric of Hitler—he was so cultured and looked
after the arts and the *bien-être*, etc.; and when I said traveling
at my age was nearly impossible, the reply was: 'Not at all—

you will have a sleeping car here in Prades and will go straight to Berlin without changing.' I wanted to add that I had rheumatism in my shoulder and had not been able to play for a long time, but they quickly changed that phase of the subject and asked if they could not see my instrument. I took it from the box and laid it on the bed for them to look at. All three went up to it and touched it with caressing fingers and admiring gestures, and asked: 'This is the instrument you have played on in Germany?' Yes—and I was thinking: How could these Germans make such a gesture when they are coldly capable of shooting and taking lives, and I was offended at the sight of them touching the wood of my cello and plucking the strings. And when they asked wouldn't I please play for them, 'just for us now,' I said no, it would be impossible—my shoulder! 'But surely you can a little?' 'No, I have tried many times and it is so disappointing that I cannot play as ever—I can't.' And the thing ended like that. But they did not go. There was silence and my expression was forbidding, to say the least. Then the commander said: 'We cannot go without having something personal of and from you,' and I understood that they had to have proof that they had been here and had tried, so I said: 'Certainly, you shall have it; what would you like?' 'A photograph of yours?' Yes, and I asked each his name and wrote 'in souvenir of your visit in my house in Prades,' with all three of their names written in. Then they went away; they had stood two and a half hours in this very room. I didn't care to accompany them to the gate: they went down and entered the car, and then did not

194

start (I was watching from the window) and suddenly they opened the door again, entered the gate, and I went out onto my gallery to see what they wanted. They said: 'Please stay where you are,' and took photographs of the house: further proof for their master. I assure you, that disagreeable experience can never be forgotten."

Casals went on: "At that time I was constantly listening to my radio—it was forbidden, and with terrible penalities. I heard Churchill, Eden, England generally. The Gestapo used to come at night to listen and find out if we were using it, but I covered the radio always with things that dulled the sound and they never found me out. On various other occasions I was visited, like so many others, by the Gestapo for the purpose of examining all the things I possessed in my one little room. Every paper, every bit of music was carefully scrutinized, my books all opened and searched for evidence of something of an incriminating nature—nothing to be found!

"One crucial moment with the Germans was when the Maquis, about one hundred men, came to Prades and attacked the Gestapo where they lived. Result, one Nazi killed, another wounded and some others hurt. A few days earlier, in a village near Prades, where the Gestapo had been received with resistance, the whole village was burned and the inhabitants killed, so that when the Maquis made this attack I was quite sure there would be shooting and that we would be among the victims. We were saved, however, by the Mayor of Prades, who presented himself at headquarters saying he would take all responsibility for the attack, and begging the German general to put the blame upon him. This was accepted."

Another critical encounter had been with the French militia, many of whom in that day were savage, vicious and cruel. A friendly young militiaman of seventeen or eighteen, who happened to be engaged to a young girl Casals knew in Perpignan, came upon a list of the men to be arrested in Prades and found that Casals was among them. The head of the militia had declared that Casals should be the first to pay for his doings—"that man was a horrid man, he wanted to shoot me"—but the young militiaman had the courage to tell his chief that he knew Casals, that everyone loved and admired him, and that they could not do this thing, it would arouse such an outcry against them. "Fortunately very shortly after this the Germans were chased from France. But then again it was horrible, for the young man this time was arrested by the Allies and went on trial in Perpignan, with many others. This was the harder to accept, because, on the radio, all these days, and in the papers, there had been constant proclamations to the young men: 'You must cooperate.' They had been obliged to follow Pétain, Laval, et al., and were later condemned to death for doing just that. I wrote a letter to the President of the Tribunal in Perpignan saying that I wanted to declare for that youth. On the day that I went there five militiamen were on trial. They put me on the bench with the prisoners, all of them young. All were finally shot but this one. He was sentenced to thirty years in prison. Later, though, he was freed, and he has since been to see me. He had saved my life!"

Casals had given concerts in Switzerland, replenishing the exchequer for the endless benevolences he practiced in Prades. Then, after the liberation of France, in December 1944, associating himself with the *bonheur* of all the French, he gave three concerts—Perpignan, Montauban and Montpellier—once more, with the disinterestedness that characterizes him, putting art at the service of just causes: the Perpignan and Montauban profits were given to the prisoners and the deported, and those of Montpellier to the benefit of its university. Everywhere the flag of Catalonia was flown at his concerts, and at the end of each he played the Catalan "Song of the Birds," the *Cant dels Ocells*, sixteenth-century jewel of Catalan folklore, in which the birds sing to the infant Jesus. At last the gates of the world were once more opened to him. A concert in Paris was suggested and fifty-six different organizations there clamored for his services. To choose between them was too much, so Paris was postponed, and it was London that had the privilege of hearing Casals first, where they welcomed him like a victorious general.

Though by 1946 the concentration camps were closed and the people scattered throughout the country, need still reigned dominant, and Casals was always ready to respond to appeals for aid and advice. The number of pleas and the calls upon his liberality were without end; most of these from people he never saw and never knew, but this did not hold him back. So as not to abandon them to their "sad luck" he con-

Manuscript of the "Song of the Birds" in Casals' handwriting

tinued living in Prades, instead of in Switzerland or any other of the countless places offered him as sanctuary. "Don't you think it would have been cruel of me to have saved myself when so many of my compatriots could not save themselves?"

Twice since leaving Spain Casals has been able to effect a meeting with members of his family—brothers, nephews, and nieces. Making the little half-French, half-Catalan Andorra (one of the two oldest and smallest republics in the world) [1] their place of gathering, the family would enter at the Spanish frontier near Puig Cerdá and go almost to the French border to meet Casals coming in from France at Escaldes.

There, in this strange country of mystery, of charm and, they say, of scandal (could it be contraband business?) Casals receives a welcome of no uncertain nature from the Andorrans. The first words of an Andorran to any friends he meets (without even taking time to give themselves *a boire*) are "Pau Casals is here— Come!" And they precipitate themselves upon the small villa of Dr. Estredella, who possesses the only possible piano in all the Republic. In the *saloncita* some twenty persons are helping to celebrate the joy of this event, and on El Mestre's right is a Dominican monk, a very warm old friend to whom he turns from time to time as he talks. In this extremely hospitable mountain country of theirs, with its wild, almost savage traditions and its constitutional rules which have not changed since the Middle Ages, the Andorrans receive their friends with *bonne table, bon vin*

---

[1] San Marino, Italy, the other.

*et bon tabac.* One can well imagine that gathering of family and friends: talk, music and talk again. His visit in 1946 was so special an event that Casals not only played his cello but—with a fervor inspired by the impelling enthusiasm of his listeners—went through at the piano the lovely melodic music of his Oratorio "La Crèche."

This Oratorio is based on a poetic setting of a Nativity Play, "La Crèche," by Juan Alavedra. Casals' predilection in composition now lies with the music of religion, and he says: "It is there, without artifice, that I find myself fully." During the last few years in Prades he has dedicated what leisure he could claim to the writing of music, composition having been one of his earliest interests.

In this most recent work of his the biblical scenes of the first Nöel are brought to life, the figures of the "Crèche" playing each in turn their role in the life of Jesus, filling in all the scenes of passion. One evening, at his upright piano, Casals played this music: he sang, he acted the various parts, waving his arms in excitement and talking in a voice that fairly trembled with the gravity of his feeling for each entrant upon the scene of that astounding night. Kings and Wise Men apostrophized, shepherds and fishermen made their salutations, angel voices intoned their benedictions; every animal singing his line—the mule (contralto), the camels (tenors), the cow (a rumbling bass), the *old* camel (basso profundo)—and above the scene a group of *angelitos* chanting in high soprano. Hosannas, lamentations, wrath, fear, purity—each witness, pitiful or strong, sensitive or hard, is vividly presented in the music, and was most graphically portrayed by the performer! When he begins to play, time does not exist for Casals, nor, indeed, for the hearers of this music. This Oratorio, and the Beethoven Ninth Symphony, with his own Barcelona Orchestra again, are the two first offerings Casals is holding in his heart for his homeland when it shall once more be free.

After the many years of anxiety felt by the friends of Casals in America, when, with the enforced silence of the occupation all letters to him remained unanswered, and terrifying rumors were being circulated as to his personal safety, relief finally came with a letter written to his friend Maurice Eisenberg, in 1944. The Germans having been driven off French territory, Casals wrote: "Now that the enemy has been forced to leave I have resumed my practicing, and you will be pleased to know that I feel that I am making daily progress." "How like Casals," as Eisenberg says, "this ever modest approach to his art; it is the key to the secret of his agelessness."

There in Prades, leading a life given to study and work, Casals was too busy each day to dwell or draw upon his rich store of memories. It was only in the evening that he could let himself be carried away by his "souvenirs"—long-ago souvenirs some of them. Despite his voluminous collection of stories, which would form an intimate history of almost three generations of great musicians, he has never had a desire to write or publish his memoirs, as many have urged him to do; though of late years he has been willing and generous in recounting anecdotes of his rich and varied life for those who can or may write them down.[2]

There are reminiscences of the many friendships he enjoyed throughout his long life: with Sir Donald Tovey, Ignace Paderewski—that other great musician who, like Casals, became during his lifetime the symbol of his country and his people—Albert Schweitzer, and Charlie Chaplin—"Charlot," the Don Quijote without lance—whose art he esteems so highly. His friendships of long ago with Edward Grieg, Camille Saint-Saëns, and Gabriel Fauré; with Colonel Piquard, the courageous defender of Dreyfus; his remembrances of *causeries* with *le tigre* George Clemenceau; his friendly encounters with Edouard Herriot, whose rich voice he recalls singing the "Creation's Hymn" during the centenary memorial services at the tomb of Beethoven in Vienna.

Albert Schweitzer, scholar, theologian, musician whom Einstein calls "one of the brilliant lights in a hopelessly dark world," Casals greatly reveres and holds in warmest friendship. At the time when they both received degrees at the University of Edinburgh in 1934, Casals gave a concert there, playing Tovey's cello concerto (with the Reid Orchestra, conducted by Tovey) and the sixth Bach Suite, after which he had to play more Bach to satisfy Schweitzer, happy and excited over hearing the Bach he had always dreamed of and never before heard. Casals had to take a train directly after the concert, and hurrying to put his cello in its box, he heard footsteps running after him down the long corridor. Turning

[2] A scholarly biography, with excellent illustrations, was published in 1941: Rudolf von Tobel's *Pablo Casals* (Botapfel-Verlag, Erlenbach-Zurich). Written in German, it has been translated into Portuguese.

he found a breathless Schweitzer saying: "We *must* have an intimacy. Couldn't we *tutoyer* each other now?" As he told of this in his room in the Villa Colette, Casals jumped up and imitated with such vigor the "pattering" steps of Schweitzer following him along the corridor that the household below, their anxiety stirred by such unaccustomed sounds from above, came rushing upstairs to see what had happened to El Maestro!

Casals sees many people in his retirement, political and musical, pupils and Catalan friends, with welcome ever ready and an interest that never flags.

Alexander Schneider, the violinist, spent several days in Prades in the early summer of 1947. He tells of Casals reading to him from various books. They talked philosophy and music, his recurrent theme being personal integrity. Here again it was clear that, as we have seen, Casals himself when young never made concessions in what he felt to be right. "One can only be a great artist if he believes in his own integrity and holds to his point." Schneider says, "Casals talked and I felt liberated. I was no longer flesh or bone but all spirit—an overwhelming experience!"

# XI

## SPIRITUAL BOYCOTT

PABLO CASALS as a prophet of resistance has become a symbol of liberty to tens of thousands of his fellow countrymen, to whom he has given the greatest moral support since the earliest days of the revolution in his country. *Moral support* is what he stresses in all his actions. Possessed by a lonely passion for ideals, his willingness to endure privation and sacrifice to achieve what he believes in has led to the utmost austerity of life for him today, and an acceptance of poverty almost monastic, Franciscan. The whole situation is for him as "a great poem, with justice and morality its theme," and he protests when anyone calls goodness a vain word. The recluse in Prades seldom uses the word conscience; for him it transforms itself into fraternity. The artist who has known how to translate his idealism into acts of practical brotherhood has become the image of independence, but he pays an enormous price for his decisions. To quote a prominent Englishman, "If the world possessed more men like Pablo Casals (and I don't speak of the musical genius) one's faith and happiness in life would be more real."

No one anywhere questions the sincerity of the man. He says he is no politician, though he lives in exile and has taken sides, and by doing so has raised acutely the whole question of the artist in relation to world affairs. Someone has rightly said that though the cello of Casals is of wood, it has more weight than if it were of iron. He uses the only long-range instrument in his power, his popularity in the world of music, as a bludgeon for Franco's back: he could not forget Guernica. Many people have tried to exploit his ideas and say he represents the extreme left. "My care is to say constantly that I belong to no party; I do not work for the Republic, but for justice. I am a patriot, a musician—representatives of various governmental interests have come to me in Prades, but no—I am not for that. Now I have the esteem of all, but if I entered government I should have all the hatred and all the trouble. This independence allows me also to express my opinion of all people—all parties—gives a power otherwise unobtainable!"

As long ago as 1937, in an interview published in Barcelona, he said: "I was born poor. My father was a man of the people—a worker; I am, therefore, a fervent democrat. Even if I have never been a politician, for music and politics do not mix, I can tell my friends in other lands that the Spanish people are absolutely blameless of this civil war provoked by the military, also that Catalonia and Spain have never been closer to one another than they are today. I cannot be neutral in the present conflict. I was born of the people, I am with the people, and I always will be with them. I believe it to be my duty to continue the work of giving concerts for the wounded and for the hospitals. If I am, in any form, part of the art of my people, I must be drafted, so to speak, to contribute to the artistic progress of Catalonia. But, apart from artistic preoccupation, my spirit is deeply democratic, and neither money nor success will ever change it. I shall never forget my humble birth, which binds me to my people, and I pity those who feel ashamed of their past, their race and their country."

Arrived at the age when Maillol worked at his most serious figures, when Tolstoy wrote the eternal pages of his *Resurrection*, when Goethe was finishing the second part of *Faust*, Casals, too, stands at the height of his artistic career with a poignancy now in his playing that these years of strain and sadness have seemed to make inevitable. His playing, on one unforgettable day in 1947 in his tiny room in Prades, of the C Major Suite of Bach, followed by the *saraband* from the C Minor Suite, haunting in its simple yet profound loveliness, and of the infinitely tender melody of the Catalonian "Song of the Birds" was of surpassing beauty, and left his two listeners deeply moved and completely inarticulate.

While his decision taken in late November 1945, to play no more in England until the liberation of Spain, and, later, not to appear in public again *anywhere* until he could play once more in his own free country, came more or less in the nature of a bombshell to the musical world—perhaps the more so because of his indisputably royal successes in all the concerts of the last year—it could not really have surprised those who had followed at all intimately the workings of his mind during these years of exile or who knew how unfalteringly he belonged to those few who, "because we had self-respect, were faithful to ourselves."

Upon his arrival in England on June 25, 1945, he addressed a message to the people of that country (London Philharmonic Post, July 1945):

I feel more than happy and privileged to have this opportunity of assuring not only my fellow musicians in this country but the entire British public of the solicitude with which I have followed all that has befallen them during these six terrible years. From my little refuge in the Pyrenees I have watched from hour to hour all the experiences through which your great country has passed, and have accorded no more importance to the many inspiring calls to action of your political and military leaders than to the countless achievements of your leading symphony orchestra and soloists during this period of ordeal. I know how you have traveled under bombardment from town to town to keep alive the cause of great music, and I know, too, how those years of trial have created millions of new listeners to the works of the great masters.

I am sure that history will always preserve the memory of how the British people kept alive the flame of civilization in wartime, and I am glad that I have lived to see that such things are possible. I was old enough when this war started and I am older still to-day, but let me say that I have lived fully during these years: I have survived all these great changes throughout the world.

I have seen the collapse of the two most hateful forms of dictatorship, and having lived through them has given me renewed strength.

He was happy to be again in London—"London, which had at first symbolized resistance and then, with America and Russia, victory, became for all of us, who for six years or more had been hanging on the words of B.B.C., the Capital of Freedom. Today it is the Capital of Hope."

On June 27 took place that extraordinary concert in Albert Hall, which was the first occasion on which Casals had played with orchestra since the Lucerne festival in August 1939, Sir Adrian Boult the conductor at both concerts. Twelve thousand listeners were in and about Albert Hall that night, and a stupendous ovation was given to the great master. Not one sole musician of the orchestra budged before the last applause of the audience had subsided—and this is saying something for those who know the habits of these blasés! Finally when he left there was a further unprecedented demonstration outside the hall, where the crowds surged about him clamoring for a speech. He could reach his car and be driven away only after the police had cleared a passage.

In his seventieth year [wrote a London newspaper] the great artist is ready to embark again on a virtuoso career with the energy and idealism of youth. As the familiar figure, unassuming, completely bald, not much taller it seemed than the cello he was carrying, picked his way through the violin desks of the B.B.C. Symphony, the vast audience at the Royal Albert Hall rose to its feet to proclaim a tumultuous welcome for the artist whose name will live not only as an artist but as a great humanist, and as a foe of tyranny.

Schumann,[1] Elgar concertos, and, as an encore, one of the Bach unaccompanied sonatas, in the interpretation of which he has set the standard for cellists the world over. Again there was that noble simplicity which marks the perfection of his art and which has given him a place apart among the world's virtuosi. From the first notes it was clear that none of the magic of his playing had been lost. . . .

He has come to symbolize the spirit of resistance among musicians. The greatness of the artist is indeed matched only by the humanity of the man. Americans and British vied with each other for the honor of bringing him over to London by plane. Eventually British Airways refused to let him pay his passage, and on his arrival he was cheered by customs officials, who refused

---

[1] After his playing of the Schumann concerto, under the direction of Sir Adrian Boult, Casals said that only twice in his life had he been so happy after a performance of that concerto—long ago with Arthur Nikisch, in Berlin, and again later in Manchester, England, with Hans Richter conducting.

to inspect his baggage so as not to keep him waiting. . . .

It has been said that no foreigner is likely to be an
ideal interpreter of Elgar; that there is something of
Englishness in the composer that must inevitably elude
any but his own countrymen. This is not true of his
work for or with an orchestra. Elgar himself found in
Richter his finest interpreter of the A flat Symphony,
and in Kreisler the most expressive soloist for the violin
concerto; we may be sure that he would have entrusted
Pablo Casals with the cello concerto, knowing that
even its most subtle native qualities would be fully
comprehended and conveyed. On this occasion the
proof was clear to every hearer. Casals brought to
strenuous passages full eloquence and a golden tone,
yet it was in the deeply meditative sections where his
playing was most touching, for it reached to an Elgarian
mood of wistfulness that few artists now understand;
why is it that few modern solo performers are patient
enough?

The Elgar concerto, one of the most successful of Casals'
recordings, was recorded at this performance.

On November 13, 1945, he gave the first Paris performance
of the concerto, at a special concert in the Salle Pleyel to
mark both the forty-seventh anniversary of his first engagement with orchestra in that city and his initial appearance
there since the war. It was the same thing: unbridled enthusiasm, and after the concert a *cola* of the most distin-

guished personalities of the Paris world waiting to shake hands with him and offer their felicitations. The director of the Salle Pleyel, accompanying him to his car, said: "Never, Maître, has our Salle—has Paris, indeed—seen a manifestation comparable to this of tonight." Reports from Paris state that as a result of Casals' performance, French cellists have evinced a keen desire to study the Elgar and perform it themselves; and Parisian musicians have taken note of Casals' advice to make themselves more familiar with the many fine works composed in England during this century which are still comparatively unknown in France.

It was in Paris in November 1945, too, that a writer on the *Cité Soir* met with two friends of Casals and in great excitement said: "*Le Maître est à Paris!*" "Where is he exactly—can we see and talk with him?" and the answer was: "I will take you—we will salute him this evening." Was he at some grand palace? Not at all. They went that early evening to a Spanish orphanage in the Avenue Bineau in Neuilly. There, in an obscure corridor (there had been a breakdown of electricity) they found Casals surrounded by children, who called him papa. "Le Maître said to us: 'Each one of these little heads represents a tragedy.' We wanted to have a photograph of this communion between unhappy infancy and the great musician, but—no light! We tried in vain to use the headlights of our motorcar. As he was leaving, the children redoubled their overflowing expressions of feeling, and he embraced them all, one by one. It was a typical picture of Casals." Casals tells of his surprise and deep emotion at finding himself surrounded by a group of these sad-eyed youngsters at Austerlitz Station, where, as he was leaving Paris after a concert given for the benefit of this refuge in Neuilly which he had helped to found, they had come to testify to their gratitude.

During that summer visit to England enthusiasm was revealed everywhere in a fashion seldom seen in that country, and all the press wrote of Casals. He gave a recital in the Cambridge Theatre in London, with Gerald Moore, pianist, with whom he also played at the Town Hall in Chelsea. He played in Sheffield with the Hallé Orchestra under the direction of Barbirolli; and in Chester Cathedral (in aid of a British war organization connected with music-making) on which occasion one newspaper wrote (July 6, 1945): "The sense of esthetic pleasure was deepened by the beauty of the noble architecture. When the music played in such surroundings matches their solemnity by its own greatness, only the most insensitive listener could fail to be uplifted by an art that is no less sacred because it is expressed without the help of sacred words; and it was greatness of inspiration in the music of Bach, and in the performance of it, that held the audience."

Outside of his concerts, recitals, and rehearsals he gave interviews, received visitors, and attended receptions, one given by the Basque community after the Cambridge Theatre concert, another in the mayor's office after the Town Hall concert in Chelsea, followed next day by a big one arranged for him by his fellow exiles of democratic Spain, at the Spanish Institute in London, which was the occasion for speeches, with the press represented. After this last (July 11, 1945) he went on to the B.B.C., where, before an invited audience, he broadcast directly to Spain, his first words to friends in his faraway land since his expatriation. After speaking, he played a new work by Roberto Gerhard and the Catalan "Song of the Birds."

Usually Casals responds to great enthusiasm with composure; he is seldom agitated before crowds, and he did not lose his sang-froid even when the Gestapo confronted him, but on this occasion he was so moved he hardly knew what he was doing. He tried on several pairs of glasses before he found those needed for reading his speech. Finally he began to speak, but his voice was smothered and indistinct, his eyes wet with tears—he was for a moment almost incapacitated. Suddenly he picked up his pipe, pulled at it furiously for a few seconds, then collected himself. He said:

> I want to express in brief words my thanks to the B.B.C. which has organized this session and has allowed me to finish this broadcast to Catalonia with some words of salutation to my faraway friends.
>
> I have come to England from my retirement in the shadow of Canigou, the other side of the Pyrenees, and first want to convey my gratitude to the English people for the cordial and enthusiastic way in which I have been received, these British people who have shown such civic conscience and heroism in meeting the sufferings of the war, even during those difficult hours when they were alone in the fight. They merit the admiration and love of all men who care for liberty and

justice, and we continue to expect from them the consolidation of the peace and the moral reconstruction of Europe.

In addressing to you these words from the heart of London my thoughts go to all those Catalans who have heard us here, and to those in our own good land of Catalonia. I would like to think that when, by the miracle of the waves, our ancient melody—*Cant dels Ocells*—reaches you these sounds may be like a suave echo of the nostalgia we all feel for Catalonia. The sentiment which holds us together, and makes us proud of being native sons, must make us work together— even those who in a moment of uncertainty and vacillation perhaps have had doubts—like brothers united in the same faith, and with the same hope for a tomorrow of peace, when Catalonia will again be Catalonia.

In October 1945—England again. He played in Manchester, Nottingham, Edinburgh, Reading, Brighton, another Cambridge Theatre recital, this time with Dame Myra Hess, a second Albert Hall engagement and finally Liverpool: this last and the Reading concert considered by the critics the high-water mark of all his performances. The proceeds of this tour, a round sum of £1,000, were given entirely to the Benevolent fund of the R.A.F. "My small contribution to the cause of this nation I so much admire." Dame Myra Hess wrote him (November 8): . . . . "I cannot find words to express the joy and honor I have had in playing with you. It has been one of the deepest experiences of my life. If I can ever shape a phrase as you do, that would be my testimony of gratitude! For so many years I have carried the sound of your playing in my ears, and now you have reminded us again of the supreme power of Beauty and Truth. I thank you with all my heart, and my prayers and wishes go with you."

During the crowded days of this last visit to England he was also guest of honor at the Royal Academy of Music Club and spent an evening playing chamber music at Madame Elena Gerhardt-Kohl's house, with Yehudi Menuhin and Gerald Moore, which ended at six in the morning, and in which the players enjoyed the music as much as the audience, the audience being composed entirely of personal friends to whom the works played were as household words. Menuhin wore a pajama-like loose gray woolen suit, Casals his well-worn brown cardigan, with, for much of the time, a pipe in his mouth. They played the B flat Trio of Schubert, and Beethoven's Op. 11 (the "little B flat"), also the C Minor. When Menuhin took time out to telephone to New York (he had already chatted with his wife and children in Australia that morning) Casals, determined not to let silence reign during that interval, played most of the first Bach Suite. At 5 A.M. they started on Brahms, the B Major Trio, second edition, adding the C Major by way of a coda.

Despite all the success and enjoyment in this English tour, he was tired, very tired, was feeling the strain of nights on the train without sleeping, and in his heart was deeply discouraged, disillusioned. He had waited for so long a time—"hoping always, as I do. I felt sure they [the English] would continue to work for us; it only awaits the psychological moment—but—we are impatient; strong forces are pulling the world in the wrong direction. I talked, and most of the men with whom I talked—ministers, influential people of the press, and high officials in Buckingham Palace, where I was received with every kind of consideration—showed themselves in accord with the idea of establishing a democracy in our country; but I kept reading the *Daily Telegraph*, the *Morning Post*, the *Daily Mail*, the *People* and many other papers, all saying good things of the Spanish regime and that Franco was offering refuge to fifty thousand children—this in a country in which children are dying of hunger—shameless! Under these conditions I began to think what shall be my attitude? Up to this moment I had talked with people everywhere, and in all kinds of situations, of our deception in finding that, after six years of faith in the triumph of the democracies, we were being abandoned."

Referring to this time, Dame Myra Hess wrote him (December 22, 1945): "You spoke so much of our democratic ideals. But in helping to reconstruct this bewildered world on democratic lines, this country is pledged as a matter of honor not to act independently of its Allies, and again not independently of the United Nations Organization which we are working so hard to set up. Although this may appear on the surface to be a slow process, please believe me when I tell you that a great deal is happening. Here you are looked upon as the most important Ambassador of your beloved country."

It was after the Reading concert that Casals began to dwell on the thought of making concrete his protest against England's official policy toward Spain.

The Worshipful Company of Musicians was preparing a reception in my honor and I thought that if in these moments I should accept honors in England it would appear to my compatriots that I was indifferent to their unhappiness, when the contrary is the case: I associate myself with them *completely*. That was my first renunciation; it was hard for me, but I could not be in doubt for one minute. Others followed: Oxford, then Cambridge. Before the war commenced the famous University of Oxford had entertained the idea of granting me an honorary degree and during this trip to England they proposed to find a date free for the ceremony. My Catalan friend, Dr. Josef Trueta, resident in Oxford, visited me with the object of confirming by word of mouth the putting through of this plan. I asked Dr. Trueta to please tell the directors of the university that under the present circumstances I found it, to my profound regret, an impossibility to accept the honor offered. The same thing happened in regard to Cambridge. The composer Gerhard, domiciled in Cambridge, told me that the name which figured in first place on the list of those proposed to be named *doctor honoris causa* of this no less eminent university, was mine; I begged similarly of my friend Gerhard to say to them that I would have to defer this intention until the position of England in respect to Spain be changed. Then I suspended all contracts for England for the following spring, also the magnificent proposition His Master's Voice had made me for the impressions of the eight Brandenburg concertos of Bach for orchestra, and other important works.

The Liverpool concert, November 8, 1945, proved to be, actually, the last concert Casals gave in England. In response to questions concerning the root of his actions he said: "One's actions are a part of one's existence—one feels it a duty to act, and whatever comes one does it—that's all—a very simple thing. I feel that the capacity to *care* is the thing which gives life its deepest significance and meaning."

On July 18, 1946, the tenth anniversary of the start of the Spanish civil war, Casals published in the London *News Chronicle* "Why Franco Must Go." He wrote:

I have already protested in the pages of this newspaper the damage done by Britain to the victorious cause of democracy by her refusal to cope openly with the Spanish problem. I stressed the disillusionment of the Spanish democrats and explained how Britain's incomprehensible attitude tends to drive our people to extremest solutions. I said, too, that it is the continued existence of a system which preserves intact beneath temporary disguises not only the germ but all of the aggressive and intolerant mentality of fascism against which we Spaniards, and millions of young people of all lands, have fought to the death. I say again to the British people, whom I respect and admire so much, that we feel cruelly let down—we who believed implicitly in Britain's historic and moral mission in the world—by this policy of turning a deaf ear to our just protests, by this method of ignoring our sufferings, or damping down any magnanimous impulse to help us, and of systematically postponing the solution of a problem which troubles the conscience of millions of democrats.

As you are aware, the exiles hounded out of Spain by Franco's rebellion and nazi and fascist forces represent the best elements in our country. Do not forget that it was these men who peacefully introduced the democratic republic in Spain. And it is more than likely that, in spite of the adverse circumstances of today, there will be found among them the men of Spain's tomorrow, for there are not only politicians, but artists, university teachers, poets, journalists, lawyers and magistrates among them. It is bitter for us all to think that one of the chief obstacles to our return is Britain's present policy of reticence and procrastination.

After the announcement that he would not play again the cry arose from all sides: *"Come!"* One request bore the signatures of the greatest musicians in England, another the assurance: "You will be received like a king." A workers' organization offered him theaters and concert halls; a

Jewish world organization wrote: "We suffer to see you suffer: let us show you all our affection." From Paris, New York, Moscow, Amsterdam, from Brussels, from Zurich and from Milan—from everywhere (excepting from his own country, "where my name is banned," Casals said with simple dignity) came appeals and moving salutations.

Come! And if you cannot come, good anniversary, Maître. Live long for the good of art, and above all, listen to us, for on the twenty-ninth of December we want to try and tell you how much we love you. Never has one seen anything like this, never for any other artist has the world vibrated with such intensity; and this is not only the result of fifty years of a life of artistic glory, it is above all, because no other artist has been like Pablo Casals at this moment *"une conscience du monde"* (in M. Bidault's phrase . . . ). It is because never before has one seen an artist—the most solicited, the most favored, and the most honored of today—refusing contracts and honors, fortunes and acclamations, to affirm the truth of his ideas, and showing other artists that an artist is not one who can be commercialized, whom one can hire or buy, and that he cannot, *must not*, give his life in his art until he feels and knows himself in full liberty among equals.[2]

Requests continued to pour in. One from Glasgow, where there were many who worked and fought for the republican

[2] Juan Alavedra, in *Republicain du Midi* December 28, 1946.

cause in the civil war, and who believed that the establishment of a democratic regime in Spain was not only a vital world necessity, but also the barest justice to the people of Spain:

> They feel the time opportune for bringing the urgency of this problem before the people of Glasgow and a concert by you would be a gesture to the British government of our sympathy with the republican cause, and of our conviction that our official government action in relation to the Franco regime is totally inadequate; it would give opportunity, too long delayed, for enjoying your rich musical gift; and, lastly, it would be a tribute to the devoted and self-sacrificing services you have given to this great cause. I need not say that a visit by you would be a landmark in our civic and musical history.

Also from Glasgow in February 1947, a letter:

> Your decision not to play until Spain is liberated is a tragic loss to the world of music, and must be a sacrifice the magnitude of which one can only remotely appreciate. Let me again pay humble tribute to all you have done and are doing for the sacred cause. Actions such as yours give one hope of a world where hope is sometimes difficult.

And from Reading, England:

> It would be dreadful to think we shall never hear you again, this surely cannot be true.

But Casals did not yield. Indeed, his concert at the University of Montpellier on March 10, 1947 was his last in public. He was not boycotting one country alone. Though he could still say: "I have faith in the world of tomorrow, and above all I *want* to have it," he had lost heart.

Casals had had many offers of engagements from the United States during the years of his exile. The Friends of Music in New York wrote him that if he would come for the season of 1946–47, they could assure him of "an audience the most concentrated in America on chamber music, surely happy auspices for your return here." A committee of citizens transmitted an invitation for a series of concerts under the auspices of anti-Franco elements and in aid of Casals' own great cause. In 1939 he had received from New York a contract with a blank left for him to fill in at his own figure. This he sent back, though deeply moved by its generosity. "Where save in America could such a thing happen?" Even in September 1945 he wrote to a Boston friend. "I have thought of my good friends in America, the country of liberty, at the time when we lived in fear of the caprices of the military and the Gestapo. You have combined with the English and you have saved the world as you did before [in 1914–18]. . . . Long live America and thank you." He explains the refusals that cost him such great regret: "America has done so much; please understand that the policies of your country are against my ideas for my country. I love America, but I could not go to a country which I should criticize."

Casals, alone, armed only by his unique art and his

moral force, can say no. "But," many have said, "he is not *doing* anything." They speak of the futility of giving up his concert tours when he could use the proceeds to buy more milk and food, more clothing for the sufferers of the war. They say: "Casals, citizen of the future decent world, can act, he can be above governments and movements, and he will have undying satisfaction from what he can do. The hungry children of Spain can understand succor, but not political or moral issues." And they say: "Break this self-imposed exile, Maestro, and play more gloriously than ever, not for any cause, but for the continued support of these innocents."

The question arises to what extent high example, falling on fertile soil, can influence or change the course of events. One wonders was Gandhi saint or politician? A living refutation of materialism, the fullest fire of his spiritual actions has undeniably had notable consequences. To abstain may be *action* of a very special character, and there can be also an enormous activity, spiritually, in such conduct. In a century of materialism and in a time of chaos, when traditional values seem to be going by the board; when all that is spiritual is in crisis, the force of the spirit is of an incomparable transcendency, and acts, perhaps, with greater efficacy than those forces which derive from purely materialistic impulses.

Casals' whole existence today is a protest against injustice. He puts full meaning into life, his activity of spirit revealing essential greatness of character.

# A LIST OF
# CASALS RECORDINGS

**BACH**

Violin sonata No. 3, A Minor, arr.
   cello and piano
   Casals and Blas-Net         12″ HMV-DB1404

Orchestral suite No. 3, D Major, Air    12″ HMV-DB1404

Unaccompanied cello sonatas,
   Nos. 1, 2, 3, & 6            Bach Society
                             Vols. VI, VII

   No. 4, E-flat Major           HMV-W1528/30

Komm' süsser Tod, Siloti
   Casals and Blas-Net         12″ HMV-DB1400

Adagio from Toccata, Adagio &
   Fugue, C Major            12″ V-6635

**BEETHOVEN**

| | | |
|---|---|---|
| Minuet in G, cello and piano | | HMV-DB1419 |
| Cello Sonata No. 1, F Major | | |
| Casals and Horszowski | 3 12″ | V M-843 |
| Cello Sonata No. 3, A Major | | |
| Casals and Horszowski | 3 12″ | HMV-DB3914/6 |
| Casals and Otto Schulhof | 3 12″ | HMV-DB1417/9 |
| Cello Sonata No. 4, C Major | | |
| Casals and Horszowski | 2 12″ | HMV-DB3065/6 |
| Archduke Trio, B-flat Minor | | |
| Casals, Thibaud and Cortot | 5 12″ | HMV-DB1223/7 |
| Zauberflöte, Männern | | |
| Casals and Cortot | 2 10″ | HMV-DA915/6 |

**BOCCHERINI**

| | | |
|---|---|---|
| Concerto, B-flat | 3 12″ | V M-381 |
| Sonata A Major, No. 6 | | |
| Casals and Blas-Net | 12″ | HMV-DB1392 |

**BRAHMS**

| | | |
|---|---|---|
| Double Concerto for violin and cello | | |
| Casals and Thibaud, with Orquestra Pau Casals conducted by Cortot | 4 12″ | HMV-DB1311/4 |

**BRUCH**

| | | |
|---|---|---|
| Kol Nidre, with London Symph. —Ronald | 2 12″ | V M-680 |

**CHOPIN**

| | | |
|---|---|---|
| Nocturne, E-flat | 12″ | HMV-DB966 |
| Prelude No. 15, D-flat, with Mednikoff | 12″ | HMV-DB966 |

**DVORAK**

Concerto, Czech Orch.—Szell 5 12" V M-458

Songs My Mother Taught Me
Casals and Blas-Net 12" V-7193

**ELGAR**

Concerto, BBC Orch.—Boult 4 12" HMV M-394

**FAURE**

Après un rêve, with Mednikoff 10" V-1083

**GODARD**

Jocelyn Berceuse ⸰ HMV-DB1039

**GRANADOS**

Spanish Dance No. 5, with Mednikoff 10" HMV-DA5402

Goyescas 12" HMV-DB1067

**HAYDN**

Minuet, C Major
Casals and Blas-Net 12" V-14843

Trio, G Major
Casals, Thibaud and Cortot 2 10" HMV-DA895/6

**LASERNA**

Tonadilla HMV-DA1118

**MENDELSSOHN**

Songs without Words, No. 49, cello
and piano
Casals and Blas-Net 12" V-7193

Trio No. 1, D Minor
Casals, Thibaud and Cortot 4 12" HMV-DB1072–5

**POPPER**

Chanson Villageoise 10" HMV-DA731

**SCHUBERT**

Trio, B-flat Minor
Casals, Thibaud and Cortot     4 12" HMV M-20

**SCHUMANN**

Trio, D Minor
Casals, Thibaud and Cortot     4 12" HMV-DB1209/12

**TATTINI**

Concerto, D Major, 3rd mvt.     12" HMV-DB1400

**VIVALDI**

Concerto Grosso No. 11, D Minor,
    3rd mvt.
    Casals and Blas-Net     10" HMV-DA1118

Orchestral Works
Pablo Casals, *conducting*

**BEETHOVEN**

Coriolanus Overture, London Symph.     HMV-D1409

Ruins of Athens Overture, Orq. Pau
    Casals     HMV-AW133

# INDEX

229

# INDEX